Random Ram

of a

Nonagenarian

Lynn M. Trowbridge

C000227615

Read Fox Books

First Edition published in 2016
by
Read Fox Books

ISBN 978-09932564-6-2-

Distributed by the author, 6,Harley Almshouses, Hay-on-Wye, Hereford HR3 5DZ

Email: l.trowbridge23@btinternet.com

Printed in the United Kingdom
By Powerprint,
Oxford Chambers, High Street,
Llandrindod Wells, Powys, LD1 6AG

ACKNOWLEGMENTS

My grateful thanks to Clare Cross who, with unfailing patience on her part and a certain irascibility on mine, has once again guided me through the more technical mysteries of my computer as well as helping with the thankless task of proof reading.

My thanks also to all the named and un-named people in the book for unconsciously providing me with much of the anecdotal material.

Do not get hooked on misery –
Lest you find happiness hard to bear.

Lynn M. Trowbridge

THE SLIPPERY SLOPE

There wasn't the same structure of orderliness and discipline now that had prevailed before my mother went into hospital, and I occasionally took advantage of the fact that Dad was too weak from his constant coughing to wield any real authority over me and my younger sister.

I cared and I worried and I did what I could, but I was not a saintly child and after doing homework, then a bit of housework, the thing I wanted more than anything was to go out and play with the other children in the street.

It was the winter of 1933 and shortly after my tenth birthday. I asked Dad if I could go out to play and he said 'No, it's too dark and it will soon be time for you to go to bed anyway.'

It *was* dark but not *that* late I thought, as I glanced up at the clock noisily ticking away in the middle of the mantelshelf, and other children were still outside, I argued. An earlier fall of snow had frozen hard and they were playing slides down the slippery slope of the street.

I took Muriel up to bed, read her a short story, then watched with envy from the bedroom window at the children enjoying themselves playing at slides under the light of the street gas

2

lamp. He'll never know, I thought, if I go out and join them, so I popped my head round the back kitchen door, said, 'Goodnight Dad,' then slyly grabbed my coat and a scarf off the peg in the hall, and tiptoed out of the front door.

Although small for my age, I was wiry and athletic and soon began competing with the boys to see who could slide the farthest. I ran, hard and fast, then straightened my legs, lifted my arms for balance and glided gracefully, like a statue in motion, over the frozen surface.

After a few more *goes* I heard one of the watchers exclaim, 'Du du, she should have been a boy!' I thought this the best thing anyone could ever say about me and to justify the comment, I hurled myself with even greater enthusiasm and skill down the slippery slope.

Gradually, some of the kids dispersed and disappeared into the night. I was disappointed to lose some of the admiring onlookers, but was still enjoying myself and determined to prove that I was the best slider. Then it happened. Bryn Williams, one of the older boys, came flying down behind me and knocked me off my feet. There was more hurt to my pride than physical damage to my person, but it was enough to make me decide I'd had enough of showing off, so decided I'd better get home before I was missed.

Bryn helped me to my feet, kept hold of my hand, and walked me back up the slope towards my house. I liked him and his family, so when he asked if I would like to see his den I was pleased and said, 'When?'

'Now,' he said.

'Where is it?'

'Not far from here,' he said.

Secretly flattered that this nice looking, older boy wanted to show me his den, yet with a certain chariness, I said, 'It's not over the woods is it? I don't like the woods in the dark.'

'No. It's in The Dip over the field,' he said.

The field fronted the row of houses in one of which I lived, so with only slight misgivings I said, 'I'll come, but I don't want you holding my hand,' and withdrew it from his.

I followed him over the frozen, snow covered field, becoming more uneasy with every step, until we reached the edge of a circle of low growing bushes, barely discernible in the enveloping darkness. Suddenly, above the sound of our feet crunching on frost, I thought I heard a low babble of voices, then a distinctive hiss, 'Shush. Here they come. Here they come.'

At that moment, Bryn turned to grab me and I knew I was in danger. I twisted swiftly from his grasp and fled. Fear gave wings to my feet and I ran, fast as a startled deer, not even looking back to see if I was being pursued. I didn't run straight for our front door - that would be too obvious a place to make for and I would be seen by the light of the street lamp. So I ran to the unlit lane at the back of the house. I burst open the garden gate, flung myself into the outdoor toilet and bolted myself in.

I sat there until my heart stopped pounding and I felt it safe to emerge. The next problem was to think of a way of entering the back kitchen without being seen by Dad. And deciding of whom or what I was the most scared - being caught by the boys if I made my way round to the front, or, if I tried sneaking in the back door, being caught by Dad.

Now shivering with cold after the heat of the chase, I longed for the warmth and safety of my bed, so decided being caught by Dad rather than the boys might be the better option. I cautiously opened the back door and furtively snuck in. Dad was still sitting in his wooden arm chair, seemingly asleep before the dying embers of the coal fire with the South Wales Echo resting on his lap.

The tabby cat, who was curled up in front of the kitchen grate, opened one eye, rose up, arched expansively, then sashayed his way towards me. He insinuated his body round my legs, then looked up at the door and meowed. I opened the door to let him out and looked anxiously across at Dad to see if he was still asleep.

He opened both eyes and looked almost as startled as I felt. He coughed, then wheezed out, 'Good God girl, what are you doing up?'

'Just letting the cat out Dad,' I said truthfully, then flew up to bed before his coughing would ease sufficiently for him to ask any more questions.

Once safely under the bed clothes, I thought about the past hour or so, how much I'd enjoyed the sliding, but what unspeakable things might have happened to me if I'd trustingly gone into Bryn Williams' den.

It was a salutary lesson and I resolved never, ever, to sneak out to play in the dark again. I'd already proved I was as good as the boys at sliding anyway and I could certainly run faster...or could I? Perhaps they hadn't been chasing me after all. – I would never know for sure.

OLD REMEDIES OF RADNORSHIRE

We hear so much about the shortcomings of the National Health Service these days that it might be worth taking a look at how much better, or worse we are now than in days gone by, when we did not have the benefits and advances in medicine that we now take very much for granted.

As I live on the borders of the beautiful county of Radnorshire, I have confined my research to this area, although, doubtless, many of the remedies and cures applied in the past may well have been used in other parts of Britain too.

In W.H. Howse's book on Radnorshire, we read of a complaint known as the King's Evil. This scrofulous disease was a form of tuberculosis which affected the lymphatic glands. From the time of King Edward, the Confessor, it had been believed that a touch of the King's hand could effect a cure. Queen Anne "touched" people for the disease, and, among those whom she touched was the great Samuel Johnson. No sovereign has since touched his or her subjects in the same manner, though the exiled Stuarts (both the Old and Young Pretender) claimed this old prerogative of their race.

Elsewhere, we find a transcript of an interesting document which used to be hung in Disserth Church, relating to the royal touch for the King's Evil. This was a proclamation of Charles 11, dated 9th January 1683, which it was ordered should be displayed in all parish churches.

It begins as follows: "Whereas by the grace and blessing of God, the Kings and Queens of this realm, by and for many years past, have had the happiness, by their sacred touch, and invocation of the name of God, to cure those who are afflicted with the disease called the King's Evil; and His Majesty in no less measure than any of his royal predecessors having had success therein, and in his most gracious and pious disposition being as ready and willing as any King or Queen of this realm ever was in anything to relieve the distresses and necessities of his good subjects..."

The proclamation lays down the times when those suffering from the disease may be presented. These were from the Feast of all Saints to Christmas, from Christmas until the end of March, "and then to cease till Passion Week, on account of the temperature of the season, and in respect of contagion which may happen to His Majesty's sacred person." Other times were to be proclaimed by the King. All sufferers were to bring with them certificates signed by the parish minister and church wardens testifying that they had not previously been presented.

8

After the Hanoverian Kings refused to continue the old custom, the patent medicine vendors stepped in and advertised their own "infallible" remedies for the disease. One such, in 1808 had a cure which worked equally well for the King's Evil, scurvy and leprosy, and remedies for the King's Evil were being advertised in the Hereford Journal in 1835.

A few medical notices, which appear old-fashioned to us now, would have been of interest to the Radnorshire folk to whom they were addressed.

A druggist from Birmingham advertised in the local press for a quantity of good-sized leeches. A Ross man commended in 1835 a new and improved method for "cupping" (bleeding) patients. Beecham's Pills worth a guinea a box were novel value in the 1860's.

Remedies for various ailments and mishaps were often devised by the people themselves, one of which was a cure for Hydrophobia, a condition caused by a bite from a mad dog (apparently a not infrequent occurrence in the 18th and early 19th century and which almost always resulted in death).

The professional 'Charmer' claimed to be able to cure the dog by getting it to swallow a piece of cheese on which were written the magic words: "Fury, gary, nary, gary, fuary, nary, fuary, gary."

It is presumed that the charmer himself administered the cure, but it is not recorded whether the efficacy of the charm worked on the bitten patient.

The churchwardens of Llandegley, in 1694 complained: "We have neither hospital, almshouse, nor any school in our p'ish, no doctor or physick, midwife, chirugeon." It may be assumed that such conditions were fairly prevalent in the widely scattered villages that make up the county of Radnorshire, even if there seems no other record of complaint.

In more recent times, before (comparatively) easy access to a doctor was commonplace, many people were obliged to apply their own cure for an illness and concoctions and remedies were often closely guarded secrets, it being feared that if they were revealed, they would lose their efficacy.

One of the more 'open' prescriptions was for a cure for shingles. This could be effected, according to an old Radnorshire tradition, by touching the body of a man who had eaten the flesh of eagles and the virtue in the healer was believed to last for three generations. So if you touched a man whose grandfather had eaten eagle's flesh, you could still be cured. A Major A.T.B. Rogers of Knighton, avowed that there was once a keeper named Price of Stanage Park, whose father was known to have eaten eagle's flesh and people suffering with shingles came from far and wide to touch him.

Even in the early 1900's many people in Radnorshire and probably in other remote parts, used folk remedies to deal with accidents and ailments, not so much relying on charms or magic, but a simple application of common sense and a 'gift' for instinctively knowing the practical thing to do in an emergency.

The late Mona M. Morgan recalls in her book "Growing up in Kilvert Country" how, when a child, she got an eyeful of rotting wood splinters. She was in a considerable amount of pain, but having no access to professional help, the local blacksmith, affectionately known as Daddy Lloyd and well known for his natural remedies, was called.

On being told of the problem, promptly and without further ado, he carefully took hold of her upper eyelashes and, pulling the lid away from the eye, inserted his tongue and licked out the offending material. She obtained instant relief and suffered no further problems.

In early Victorian times it is perhaps a measure of how little doctors were esteemed, when, at most large houses, they were required to use the tradesmen's entrance. Even so, their status had considerably improved since 1777 when an advertisement appeared in a local paper for "A sober, steady person to act in the capacity of Doctor, Surgeon, Apothecary and Man-midwife" to a family; he was also required "to act occasionally in the capacity of a butler, to dress hair and wigs, to read prayers occasionally and to give a sermon every Sunday evening. As a set off to these requirements, the chosen applicant was to have "Liberty to turn a penny in any branch of his profession, when not required by the family."

Up to about the year 1800 the so called *doctors* usually met with in country districts were very different from the skilled practitioners who began to emerge in Victorian times in large towns and cities.

Their surgical methods were often crude and their prescriptions primitive. The only qualification needed for them to practice was to serve a sort of apprenticeship to an already practising doctor, Thus, for instance, a surgeon setting up business in Kington in 1771 advertised that he had been a pupil of the surgeon in the town and "practised entirely in the manner" of that surgeon. He added that he cured ruptures in children and young people and made trusses for older people "which may be worn without any inconveniency". This apprenticeship for doctors was still practised in Radnorshire in the 1850's.

We may sometimes feel justified in complaining about our present system of health care, but it has certainly come a long way in my life time even, and we owe a debt of gratitude to Aneurin Bevan, who, as Minister of Health in 1948 was responsible for the inception of our National Health Service, "For the provision of dental, mental and physical care for all people and the diagnosis and treatment of illness."

We now come to expect that whatever ails us will be quickly and accurately diagnosed and efficiently treated, and anything short of the highest standard of care is no longer acceptable. But before we complain too bitterly, perhaps it's worth remembering how our forebears had to deal with their various afflictions and be thankful for the enormous strides that have been made in the care of the sick. Many of the diseases that were once a death sentence, (even in my young days), with the aid of modern medicine and the N.H.S. can now be cured and the sufferer expect to survive in good health into old age.

Retired dentist Osmond Cross

BY GUM

I was not looking forward to my visit to the dentist, when I was
to have a root filling on one of my teeth. Even the thought of
the needle going in to deaden the pain filled me with terror. I
lay in the reclining chair, hands clenched waiting for the sharp
prick, but was surprised to find that the dentist seemed to be
rubbing my gums with something which induced a mild,
tingling sensation. When I was able to talk, I asked her what
she'd been doing and she said she'd been applying a substance
to my gums to numb the sharpness of the needle going in. I
relaxed a bit and in no time at all, the work had been

completed, I hadn't felt a thing and marvelled at the advances in modern dentistry and felt glad that I didn't live in an age when anyone who had a mind could set themselves up in practice with no training.

Many of these practitioners were known as "conjurers" or "charmers" and used magic spells to cure a toothache, often including St. Peter in the words of their spells. Here are the words quoted by Edmond Owen: "What aileth thee Peter?" and Peter answered "Oh Lord, I have the toothache" and Jesus said, "be thou healed" and the toothache left him that very hour.

Even in my very young days, if the tooth was troublesome enough and the sufferer brave enough, a visit to the local cobbler was often resorted to. He did not use charms or magic words but had a more practical, if brutal way of dealing with the problem. His method was to tie a piece of thread round the troublesome tooth, securing the other end to his cobblers last, then suddenly dropping it from above the patient's head.

To extract a tooth from the lower jaw, the hapless sufferer was to lie on their back facing the door and the other end of the thread would be tied to the door handle, which was then slammed with great force. Often, however, the sheer terror of knowing what was about to happen was enough to send the pain away and the victim would plead to be spared.

I once had a conversation with Osmond Cross, a gentleman in his late eighties who had qualified as a dentist over sixty years previously, and was fascinated listening to him telling me of his experiences when he first starting practising as a dentist in Tenby, South Wales.

The surgery in Tenby was only open two days a week, the rest of the week being spent commuting by train with his cumbersome equipment, including a treadle operated tooth drill to various other parts of South Wales, spending half a day at one place, half a day at another and a whole day somewhere else.

There were no proper, purpose built surgeries in these small towns and often, some enterprising town dweller would rent out the front room of their house to various bodies. In Saundersfoot, the front room of the house was rented to the dentist on one day, the doctor the next day, the Bank following that, insurance company on another day and on Fridays to a rent collecting agency.

He recalled one occasion when he'd finished his stint at Saundersfoot, arriving at the railway station to catch the last train back to Tenby. He reached the station with no time to spare and was accosted by the Station Master, who said there was a man in the waiting room urgently needing treatment for raging toothache. Concerned that he would miss his last train, he protested that he didn't have time to spare, but the Station Master was prepared and said, 'Don't you worry about that sir, we'll hold the train up for you until you've finished.'

The tooth was extracted in the waiting room, without benefit of pain relief, whilst the Station Master held the patient down. Anxious about the welfare of the poor suffering chap, he was assured that the patient would be taken care of by the porter, who'd had previous experience in these matters and would put him on the train waiting on another platform to take him home.

He told me pregnant women were advised to have their decaying teeth removed, the theory being that the decay might poison or harm their unborn baby. Many young women ended up toothless after several pregnancies unable to afford dentures. Their beauty was obviously impaired, but their husbands weren't too bothered as it made them less attractive to other men.

For the better off, it was not unusual for a father, as a wedding present, to pay for his daughter to have all her teeth out (whether necessary or not) so that, on her wedding day, she would be looking her best in her gleaming white gnashers and, more to the point, would never have to worry about toothache again. Occasionally, this service was also purchased as a very acceptable twenty-first birthday present.

Sometimes, if there was only one person in the family with a set of false teeth, they would be borrowed by other toothless members to have their photograph taken, or attend a dance or special occasion. The mind boggles at the problems this tooth sharing must have caused.

Mr. Cross added that he now shuddered to think of the various beliefs and customs that were carried out in those early days in the name of good dentistry.

For my part, despite the well documented shortcomings of the dental service, I am glad that I live in an age when the most painful part of any visit to the dentist is the cost.

SAME MAKE – SAME COLOUR

Before I had a car of my own I would sometimes ask my boss if he would give me a lift home at lunchtime as he had to pass my door on the way to his own home. On this occasion he said he needed to stop to get some cigarettes so he pulled up outside the tobacconists. I was on the nearest side so I volunteered to jump out and get them.

On emerging from the shop I tried to open the car door but it was locked. After a few tugs the driver stretched his arm over to unlock it. I tossed the cigarettes into his lap, but before getting in I had to remove a map from the passenger seat, so I picked it up and threw it onto the back seat, thinking, whilst I did it: How silly of him to put something on the seat when he knows I've got to sit on it.

Then I plonked myself down and we sat...and sat. 'Come on,' I urged impatiently, 'what are we waiting for?'

'Where would you like to go?' he enquired.

'Home of course,' I said, 'where else?'

'And where is home?' he asked.

Convinced he'd suddenly lost his senses, I turned to give him a questioning look.

'Oh, my God!' I exclaimed. 'I'm so sorry – I'm in the wrong car.'

It must have been an odd sight for passers by to see one highly embarrassed woman staring at two grown men clutching each other for support as they staggered around the pavement laughing uncontrollably.

THE PERILS OF MOTORING
MY FIRST LONG JOURNEY

I bought my first car in 1950 when I was twenty-eight. It was a 1936 Ford Eight and already about fourteen years old, but it was described in the advertisement as a "good runner." Well, if it runs as well as me, I thought, it'll be fine. So I bought it, tarted it up a bit, learned to drive it, passed my test in it, treasured it and loved it like nothing I'd ever owned before.

After passing my test on 17th December 1950 I was anxious to show the car off to my sister, who was living in Kent and with whom I'd arranged to spend Christmas. All my friends said I must be mad to drive all that way when I'd only just passed my test and as for navigating my way through London – well! (No Motorways or M25 in those days). I told them I'd have to do it one day, so why not now.

I had to work up until lunchtime on Christmas Eve so was not able to make an early start. It was a bitterly cold day and the car was not fitted with a heater, so I put on the warmest clothes I had, which happened to be my riding gear with the thick serge, balloon style jodhpurs, riding boots and a thick woollen roll neck sweater. I also had a small, flat paraffin heater, which I put on the floor on the passenger side of the car and off I set at about 1pm on my hundred and sixty odd mile journey.

Someone had written down the route for me and that was all right whilst it was still daylight but come nightfall, there being no interior light in the car, I couldn't read it anyway. So on reaching London I had to stop every few miles to ask the way and everybody seemed to give me different instructions, or was it me just not listening properly. Whatever, cars behind me would get impatient and start hooting and I would feel obliged to move on whether it was in the right direction or not.

At one stage I came to a crossing being controlled by a policeman and as I approached he put his hand up for me to stop. My brakes weren't very good and I shot straight underneath his arm before coming to a halt. I looked up at him in sheer terror, but to my relief, he smiled down on me and said, 'Nearly got me didn't you.'

I thought to ask him directions, but he was so busy controlling the traffic, that when he beckoned me to move I moved straight on. I knew I was being a nuisance to other drivers because I was going too slowly and never sure which lane I should be in, or which way I should turn, so they would either hoot me and send my blood pressure soaring, or deliberately cut me up after managing to squeeze past me. I'm sure they would have been shocked if they could have heard the stream of un-lady like obscenities I muttered from time to time..

To add to my woe, the paraffin heater gave out no appreciable heat. All it did was give me a headache from the fumes, obliging me to turn it off and open the window to let out the evil fumes, making me colder even than I already was.

By some miracle of misguided navigation, I eventually found myself almost out of London and on the Rochester Way, winging my wheels towards the Isle of Sheppey. It was only then that I had any sense of it being Christmas Eve, so I started singing carols to keep my spirits up. Midnight came and went and I wished Jesus a happy birthday and thanked him for bringing me safely through London, and even said how sorry I was about all the swearing.

Away from the big city, the roads were practically deserted and in the black, freezing night, I now began to feel an overwhelming sense of utter aloneness. What would I do if the car broke down and where would I get help.

It was a relief when I at last reached the Kings Ferry Bridge that connected the island to the mainland, but my relief quickly turned to horror, when, as I drove over it, the most awful clatter rent the still night and I thought the engine was about to blow up. When the clattering stopped, as suddenly as it had started, I was surprised to find I was still moving. Then I remembered it was a loose, wooden slatted bridge, built to be lifted to form an inverted 'V' to let shipping through, and it was the loose planks that had made the almighty clatter as I drove over them.

I wended my way along narrow, winding roads, flanked on either side by ditches until, at last, I reached my destination at Minster-on-Sea at 1.30am. I knocked on the door and Muriel popped her curler clad head out of the bedroom window and said,

'You're late – I thought you were never going to make it.'

Not a very welcoming greeting, I thought, after all I'd gone through to get here but I soon cheered up after a sandwich, a chat and a nice hot cup of tea, not to mention the warm glow that comes with a sense of achievement – no matter how trivial.

ON TOW

My second car was a 1939 Ford Eight, a slight improvement on the first, and at least it had a sloping roof instead of the very dated straight back. However, like my previous car, it had transverse springing and although the previous owner had had an 'anti-roll bar' fitted, under certain conditions it still wasn't all that stable. So on the rare occasions that I managed to overtake another vehicle, I had to be careful not to pull in too quickly as the offside wheels were likely to lift and leave me driving on the nearside two wheels, which was quite scary.

Not nearly as scary however, as the time I was given a tow by a huge lorry. I'd driven through a ford in Kenilworth which I'd done many times before without any trouble, but on this occasion it was deeper than usual, the engine got wet and I was stuck. Some schoolboys on the bridge, obviously enjoying watching the spectacle of stranded motorists, gallantly waded into the water in their wellies and pushed me out. But the car wouldn't start so I lifted the bonnet and tried drying the leads to the sparking plugs.

Whilst doing this a large lorry pulled up and offered help but the car still wouldn't start so he offered to give me a tow. I gratefully accepted his offer and said I would hoot him loudly when the car got going under its own power..

He hooked me up and went roaring off at a rate of knots and it wasn't long before my car jerked into life and I no longer needed to be towed. I sounded my horn and flashed my lights and gave despairing, futile shouts at him to stop, but he sped on and on until we careered out of Kenilworth, round a traffic island and onto the main Birmingham highway, with me still hooting and flashing whilst swaying perilously from one side of the road to the other.

Stricken with terror, I was also furious because I thought the lorry driver must be absolutely mad racing along so recklessly with me on the end of a piece of string. My sister always used to say that if ever I had a bad car accident I would die either singing hymns or swearing. Well, I knew for sure now that I would die swearing.

I don't think I'd ever expected my ancient little Ford Eight car to do much more than forty miles an hour and here we were, doing at least sixty, the while I tried to keep control of the steering, hoot my horn, flash my lights and bawl expletives like a demented fish wife. When I'd finally given myself up to the inevitable, I calmly prepared to meet my fate, and before breathing my last I stopped the swearing and muttered fearfully, "Into thy hands oh Lord, I commend my spirit.'

Shortly after this the lorry seemed to be slowing down and eventually came to a halt in a lay-by. I was so relieved at still being alive that I had no cross words of reproach for the driver, meekly saying I thought he was never going to stop and hadn't he heard me hooting.

He apologised profusely, explaining he'd completely forgotten he had me in tow and couldn't hear me hooting above the noise of his engine. Then he added that he hoped he hadn't given me too much of a scare.

'Oh, I *wasn't* scared,' I lied with false bravado. 'I just wondered if you were ever going to stop and when you did, if I'd manage to get back to Kenilworth in time for my dental appointment. I think I'll just about make it and thank you ever so much for helping me,' I said lamely.

I didn't make it to the dentist in time but wasn't entirely sorry. I'd had enough terror for one day!

GOOD RUNNER – CARELESS DRIVER

I arranged to visit a friend who'd recently moved to Clapham, in London. She'd given me instructions on how to get to her new address, but after a journey of about ninety miles, and within striking distance of my destination, I suddenly lost my way, so I stopped the car and asked a passer by if he could direct me to the road I was looking for.

'You've come past it luv,' he said. 'Turn round when you can then take the third turn on the right and the second on your left and you're there.'

I followed his instructions to the letter, but on turning into the second left, I was a bit alarmed to see a builders' lorry driving towards me in the middle of the road and making no attempt to move over. I had to stop and the lorry stopped and we sat, angrily eyeballing each other.

Then I got out of my car and strode towards him to ask him what he thought he was playing at. At the same time the burly driver leapt from his cab and came running towards me. I thought he was going to hit me, but he ran straight past me and when I turned, it was to see him running after my car which was slowly rolling backwards down the incline.

Feeling a bit of a fool, I thanked him for rescuing my car and then felt even more foolish when he said, 'You can't come up 'ere luv, it's a one way street.'

SPEEDING TICKET

I've had two or three speeding tickets in the past. Nothing serious, usually just a few miles over the speed limit in a built-up area, which is the normal hazard of being a modern motorist.

This time it was different. I was in my 89th year and one day a brown envelope plopped through my letter box. Always pleased to have some mail, no matter the source, I picked the envelope up and put it on the table beside my breakfast plate and would open it over a cup of tea.

I was shocked when I did get round to opening it to discover it was from the Cardiff Constabulary to say I'd been clocked doing 92 miles per hour on the A465. Well, I wasn't so much shocked at the speed but at the fact that I'd been caught doing it! I remembered that on the date indicated I was travelling back from a visit to my niece in Neath, to my home in Hay-on-Wye. I also remembered that I was following a van, which seemed to be driving very slowly on the practically empty dual carriageway, so I put my foot down and shot past it. Some distance further on, I glanced at my speedometer and realised I was doing 95 miles per hour, so I eased back on the throttle to the accepted speed limit of 70 m.p.h.

So I knew I was guilty, but terrified, for the notification said I was to appear at Cardiff Magistrates Court on a given date and I had to fill in a form of how I wished to plead. I naturally filled it in at once pleading guilty and posted it off straight away in order to avert the possible dire consequences if I didn't.

I told a few friends what had happened and instead of showing concern for me, most of them thought it hugely funny that a lady of my advanced years should be had up for driving at this speed anyway. Then there were others, who, after seeing the funny side of it, warned me of all the possible consequences viz: My driving licence would be revoked; I'd have a very heavy fine; if I wanted to get my licence back they would probably make me take another driving test – but even then – I might not be able to get insured again. Oh, the misery of it – and still they laughed, although I failed to see the funny side of it.

There ensued days of worry and anxiety: I would lose my independence without my car, be unable to do my own shopping, visit friends or go out to lunch unless I was taken. And what about the fine - would that be utterly crippling? And besides all that, I didn't know Cardiff and how was I going to find the Court I was supposed to appear at anyway?

A couple of weeks later another official looking brown envelope plopped through my letter box. I seized it and rushed into the toilet to open it. (Acute fear has always affected my bowels). With trembling fingers I tore open the envelope, my eyes popping out of their sockets with nervous tension. I read the contents, read them again, then leapt up from the toilet and whooped with relief.

The communication said that if I agreed to pay a fine of £60 and send my driving licence to the DVLC to be endorsed with three penalty points, no further action would be taken. I floated on air to the Post Office with my cheque and driving licence, then floated back home without a care in the world.

And I didn't mind in the least when people laughed at the idea of an eighty-nine year old lady being done for speeding at 92 miles an hour. I could even share the joke myself now, but will always be especially careful to keep within the speed limit when driving on the A465 in future.

UNJUST JUSTICE

A friend has a husband who, when driving, frequently ignores the speed limit signs, but has never been caught. She was always reminding him to observe the limits, but he almost always ignored her and would drive at whatever speed suited *him* and damn the restrictions.

On this particular occasion they were off for a few days' holiday and, as usual, despite his wife's entreaties to slow down, he continued to ignore the signs, telling her crossly, to stop nagging.

Eventually, this led to a bust-up, culminating in him pulling into a lay-by and telling her to drive the bloody car herself, which she did, and they continued their journey in irked silence.

A few days after arriving home she was dusting her husband's desk when she noticed a green, official looking document lurking beneath some other papers. She picked it up and discovered it was a summons for speeding, which he'd already filled in, pleading guilty.

Serve him right, she thought. The sneaky so-and-so wasn't even going to tell me about this. Then she examined the summons more closely before putting it back where she found it. The day wore on and as it seemed obvious he was not going to confess to the summons, she decided to confront him before it was too late.

'Why didn't you tell me you had a summons for speeding then?'

'Because,' he said, 'I knew you'd nag and tell me it served me right.'

'Did you study the form thoroughly before you filled it in?' she enquired.

'Of course I did,' he retorted irritably, 'and there you go again, nag – nag – nag!'

'Well,' she said, 'you obviously hadn't studied it closely enough.'

'And what exactly do you mean by that?' he demanded.

'Because,' she replied, 'you weren't driving the car on that particular stretch – it was me.'

A quick phone call to the appropriate authorities explaining the situation resulted in a new summons being issued. My friend was fined £60 and given the option of attending a driving course as an alternative to having her licence endorsed. She elected to do the course and said she actually quite enjoyed it.

FAST LADY – SLOW TRAFFIC

The traffic moved more slowly than I could walk. Each time it caught up with me I noticed the same driver consulting a map. I tapped on his window and asked if I could help him.

'No', he said with a scowl.

How rude, I thought, he deserves to be lost.

Then I became hot with indignation when it dawned on me what he thought he'd refused.

BEWARE OF FLIPPANCY

In my late fifties, I was walking back to my car when I heard a series of 'wolf whistles'. I couldn't imagine they were for me and resolutely ignored them. The whistles persisted and my curiosity got the better of me, so whilst inserting the key in the door lock I chanced a glance round.

There stood a middle-aged man, grinning broadly, who said, 'I hope you didn't mind my bit of fun.'

'Oh no,' I said flippantly, 'I'm grateful for anything these days.'

'So am I – so am I,' he enthusiastically agreed.

NOVEL CHAT UP

It was my lunch break and I went to my usual café and sat at my favourite table in the window, where I could relax over a light lunch and the Daily Mail.

Shortly, a gentleman came in, looked around at all the empty tables, then instead of selecting one, came over to my table and asked if he could join me. I was not pleased, but grudgingly said 'yes' the while I looked meaningfully around at the empty tables, before burying my head in my newspaper.

He tried to make conversation, to which I made only perfunctory replies, but, nothing daunted, he suddenly thrust his hand forward and said, in an unmistakably Irish accent, 'My name's Patrick, what's yours?'

I gave him a withering look before answering, 'Lynn, if you really must know', then stuck my head back in my newspaper.

The meal arrived and I looked up to thank the waitress.

Patrick looked straight at me, then said, 'May I congratulate you Lynn?'

'On what?' I said, without interest.

'On your recent elevation to my acquaintance.'

I laughed and said that was the most novel chat-up line I'd ever heard.

''Twas worth it! Twas worth it,' he said, 'just to see yer lovely smile.'

I thawed, and laid my newspaper aside.

A BACK-HANDED COMPLIMENT.

I recently bumped into a lady of my acquaintance whom I hadn't seen for some time and said, 'Hello, how are you?'

She did a double take, then, with a look of surprise, exclaimed, 'Oh, it's you. You *do* look nice – I almost didn't recognise you.'

I laughed as I said, 'Are you trying to tell me I don't usually look very nice then?'

'No, it's not that,' she back-tracked. 'It's my eyes, I don't see very well. I'm waiting to have my cataracts done.'

MISTAKEN IDENTITY

A friend (whose mental health was not quite what it had been) and I went to Mid-Wales for a few days holiday. The scenery was spectacular and I took lots of photographs. When they were developed I showed them to Maggie, who, after looking at them, pointed to one and said, 'That's a lovely photograph of you standing by the waterfall.'

Puzzled, because I knew she hadn't taken any photographs, I looked at the photo indicated and said, 'That's not me, it's you.'

'Oh!' she exclaimed in horror. 'Isn't my hair a mess and don't I look fat!'

THE CHRISTMAS SPIRIT

Some years ago, when I lived in a flat, my friend John bought me a C.D. for Christmas with choruses from Handel's Messiah on it. Being a great lover of Handel's music – especially the Messiah – I was very pleased with the present, and to show my appreciation, played it immediately, occasionally joining in with the sopranos.

I think it was more than John could stand and he pleaded, 'Turn the sound down. What about the neighbours?'

I was getting carried away and un-characteristically spread my arms and said, 'Oh, to hell with the neighbours!'

'Oh yes,' he grinned. 'The season of goodwill to all men and to hell with the neighbours is it?'

IRRELIGIOUS SLANTS ON RELIGION

GENESIS

Said Eve to Adam, 'I'm speaking to thee.'
'Who Me?'
'Well who else do you think it could possibly be?
Now I want you to come and look at this tree,
Don't you think it looks quite extraordinary?'

Adam gazed at the tree suspiciously,
Then to Eve he said, rather cautiously,
'That's not the tree that the fruit thereof
We're not supposed to eat my love –
is it?'

'Well I think it might just happen to be
For the serpent pointed it out to me
Saying, 'Eat of this fruit for it's really good
And get Adam to taste if you possibly could –
There's no harm in eating a tasty apple
If with your conscience you can grapple.'

So I'm tempting you, my love, my sweet,
Come taste of this fruit I do entreat.'

'I will my love, you've won me round,
Let's eat of these apples that here abound –
Shall we?'

So they ate of the fruit forbidden by God,
Then Eve said to Adam, 'You're looking most odd,
Do cover yourself with a leaf from a tree,
The sight of you naked is most unseemly.'

'Oh really,' said Adam, feeling very perplexed,
'Whatever are you going to say to me next,
And you're a fine one to say I look queer,
Have you looked at yourself just lately my dear?'

'Oh God! We'll be in trouble for sure
Now that it seems we're no longer pure.
Our egregious crime is now disclosed
For our sinful bodies we've exposed.

I'd never have done what I did had I known
That for my transgression I'd have to atone.
You tempted me Eve, that you cannot deny,
With your wishes I felt I just had to comply –
Didn't I.'

'It's all *my* fault now, is it?' Eve replied.
'Well I'll tell you for nothing it's the serpent who lied.
But now we have sinned from God we must hide,
Make ourselves scarce and cover our pride.'
'Must we?'

'You can't hide from me,' said God all affronted,
As the two miscreants he furiously confronted,
'You are no longer welcome in Paradise,
In disobeying me you've now become wise.
So keep your knowledge but get out of this place.'

Like sad refugees, they left in disgrace.

And that is how human life began,
When Eve tempted Adam, and he became man.
Is it?

OH! LEVITICUS

O Leviticus, Leviticus,
What have you to say to us
to educate the people in God's law.
And if we flout your stringent rules
or make ourselves look perfect fools
Will God our father love us less or more?

In chapter eighteen – twenty two,
if man should lay with man it is taboo,
He's an abomination in your sight;
must we then with sword him smite
And does this law apply to women too?
O Leviticus, Leviticus, please tell us,
what are we supposed to do?

A bull is burned as sacrifice to God,
who thinks it smells quite nice;
But our neighbours think the practice quite obscene,
So do we bawl and shout them out
or ask them nicely not to so mean?
O Leviticus, Leviticus,
what will our neighbours think of us?

According to twenty-five forty four –
a man can buy slaves males females, galore
Provided they're heathens from another nation.
Does this smack of discrimination?
But there it is writ in the law of the land,
so who will dare to stay my hand.
O Leviticus, Leviticus,
what will our slaves all make of us.

I have friends who work on the Sabbath Day,
but in Exodus it doth clearly say:
For this wicked crime we must put them to death.
Are we obliged to do what it saith?
O Leviticus, Leviticus,
I'm sure God won't be pleased with us.

Look at Leviticus eleven verse ten,
where we see there are more laws written when
It's forbidden to eat the flesh of shell fish,
which for many may seem a nice tasty dish,
But I, for one, shall ignore this behest
and eat up my scampi along with the rest.
O Leviticus, Leviticus,
what will our Maker make of this?

We come to Leviticus twenty-one twenty,
which bars the altar those flawed of eye.
On reading this topic, I admit I'm myopic,
but can you explain to me why: A man who is scabby,
broken-boned or has scurvy,
in the sight of God is deemed unworthy?
O Leviticus, Leviticus
what will our Maker make of us?

In Leviticus nineteen-twenty-seven,
there's many a soul will be banned from heaven
If from their temple they trim their hair –
but do you think this strictly fair,
For many men have no locks to trim –
are *they* all banned from meeting Him?
O Leviticus, Leviticus,
do clarify this law for us.

Another law in the law of the land –
if we sleep with an in-law, how do we stand?
Look at Leviticus twenty-fourteen
and study it carefully where it'll be seen
we must burn them with fire, set them alight,
then gaze on vengeance keen with delight.
O really good people all spotless of sin,
let's be glad and rejoice whilst doing 'em in!

In Leviticus twenty-four ten sixteen it says:
whomsoever should curse or blaspheme,
Let the people take hold of him, stone him to death.
That's what the law of Moses saith.
So again, all good people untainted with sin,
lay hands on wrong-doers and do 'em all in!
O Leviticus, Leviticus,
may God have mercy on all of us.

WHAT IF CHRIST WERE BORN TODAY

So, Mary, notwithstanding the exceptional,
Immaculate circumstances of your conception,
it is understood you have no place to go.
You are not married to this man
and neither has a maternity bed been arranged.

I also understand no mid-wife is attending you
and that you are presently sleeping in a stable –
with animals to share.

Well, I'm very sorry my dear,
but I'm afraid, for the time being,
your baby…
will have to be taken into care.

Being a person with a practical attitude to life, I have some
sympathy for Martha in the biblical story of Martha and Mary
(Luke 10. 38 – 42) which inspired me to write the following
poem.

SISTERS

Banging about in the kitchen
silently seething:
Chickens don't stuff themselves
potatoes don't peel themselves
greens don't wash themselves
and dishes don't mysteriously
just land on the table.

But no one pays any attention to me
buzzing about like a blue-arsed fly,
bringing in dishes
taking out dishes
washing up dishes –
sweat and tears of fury and frustration
mingling with the blissed out bubbles
in the washing up bowl…

Whilst they chat about this and that –
I lurk briefly in the doorway
trying to catch a snatch of what they say,
the while Mary stoops over Him
tenderly washing his feet,
whilst giving ear
to his sapiential words.

He raises his head briefly
from staring lovingly

at her flowing, raven locks.

'Chill out Martha,' he says
in soothing tones
as he catches my killing look.
'Be more like your sister Mary,
she has chosen the better part.'

'Too right she has,' I mutter,
as I flounce back to the kitchen
to make yet another cup of tea.

'I wish someone would wash
 my bleeding feet
and that's the Gospel truth.'

CONSEQUENCES

The preacher stood before us
His body rigid with righteousness,
Fierce eyes piercing our fear shot-souls,
A messenger of the Almighty
Conveying grave news:

There are consequences for Mortal Sin –
Those who die in this dreadful state
Will suffer everlasting torment
From the fearsome flames of hell,
The fury of which will never be enough
To purge your sinful souls.

The threatening words bounced of the stark,
White-washed walls of the little Welsh Chapel
Battering the very core of our being.

A devout worshipper, red with guilt,
Mopped his sweating brow,
Coughed a little, composed himself, then
Widened his eyes in mock innocence.

God knew differently of course –
And so did I…

'Amen', thundered the preacher.
'Amen', soughed the congregation.

Then we all sang: *Jesu, lover of my soul,*
Let me to thy bosom fly.

WHAT'S IN A NAME

Whilst shopping recently with a friend we saw a pretty, smiley baby in a carrycot. She seemed to be looking at us and I peered more closely into the cot, smiled at the baby, then looked up at the person in charge and said, 'What a lovely baby.'

'Yes,' she said. 'I'm her grandmother and her name is Bethan, Rose, Ernestine.'

'Bethan,' I repeated. ''That's a lovely old Welsh name.'

'Yes,' said the grandmother, 'my daughter called her that after her father's mother and she gave her the name Ernestine because if they'd had a boy they would. have called it Ernest, but don't ask me where Rose came from for I've no idea.'

She thought for a moment, whilst we continued to goo over the baby, then added, 'Ah - perhaps the *Rose* comes from WAITROSE - there's a lovely big store in Abergavenny where they live.

WHEN A SMILE IS WORTHWHILE

One of the few voluntary missions I have left in life is to hand out the hymn books to people who attend our local church on a Sunday morning and greet people as they come in. On one occasion I spoke with three people, two of whom were middle-aged and one considerably older. They said they were on holiday, that they were sisters and the other lady was their mother who was in her nineties and very deaf. To make her feel included in the brief chat I turned to her, smiled, and carefully enunciated a few words.

She grasped my hands with both of hers, held my gaze and said, 'I'm very deaf and don't always hear the words, but I can see a smile and that is worth all the words I miss.'

49

CENTENARIANS

MAY STRATFORD

(1893 – 1993)

So far, I've only known two people in my life who lived to be a hundred. The first one was called May and was the mother of Rose - a friend of mine. She had never married, having been in service all her life, but somehow managed to give birth to Rose at the age of forty-six and, despite pleadings from her daughter to reveal the identity of her father, she would only say 'It doesn't matter,' and took the mystery with her to the grave.

When May got too old and frail to live independently, Rose took her into her own home to live with her and her friend, where she settled happily, and was no trouble at all, for she was seldom unwell and was always ready to help around the house with any minor chores.

When my friends went on holiday I would have May come and stay with me, but I was not entirely happy about this as I was always in dread that she might die in the night, or if she didn't die in the night, she might fall coming down the stairs in the morning. It was a responsibility I could have wished to be spared, but I did my best to remain cheerful and positive.

Fortunately, neither of these things happened and she safely negotiated her passage to her 100th birthday. Rose threw a party for her and invited lots of people and nearly everyone who arrived swooped on her, looked into her face, and said, 'Happy birthday May. Have you had your telegram from the Queen?'

May must have got a little tired of hearing this, for when one young lady leaned over her and patronizingly said, 'Happy birthday May – have you had your telegram from the Queen?' she said, 'Happy birthday to you too – have you had yours yet?'

Lots of drink flowed, but despite Rose's entreaties to her mother to have a celebratory drink, she resolutely refused. Finally, Rose said, 'Oh, come on mother, why won't you have a small sherry, after all, it *is* your birthday?'

'No thank you dear,' replied May. 'If I start drinking alcohol now, I might get a taste for it.'

About six months later May caught a very bad cold. I went to see her and said I hoped she'd feel better in the morning.

She gave me a wan smile and said, 'I'm too old to feel better dear,' and died in her sleep that night

DOLLY EAGLES
(1912 – 2012)

Dolly, despite her great age with all its attendant infirmities, was full of enthusiasm for life and for people and always ready to go on an adventure of some sort or another. In fact, she used to wear me out sometimes with her indefatigable enthusiasm for 'doing things' especially when she would persuade me to drive her to Hereford on a shopping trip. We would wander round department stores to look for a dress or a skirt or whatever she thought she wanted, but being partially sighted, I had to describe everything to her.

'Now, I'm looking for a new dress,' she would say, seizing a skirt. 'What colour is this?'

'That's a skirt, Dolly,' I would say.

'Oh. I could do with a new skirt. What colour is it?'

'Green. But they have other colours in the same style.'

'What size is it?'

'Size 14.'

'Too big.'

'How much is it?'

More peering without my glasses, which I've forgotten to bring, so I wearily say, 'Nearly £25.'

'Ooh! I'm not paying that for a skirt. I'll never live long enough to wear it out. Where are the dresses?'

'Here they are Dolly, we're standing in front of them.'

She grabs the first dress on the rail. 'What colour's this?'

'Red.'

'I never wear red – the colour doesn't suit me. What size is it?'

'Size 10.'

'That might fit me – shall I try it on? How much is it?'

'I think is says £45 something, or it might be £43. or maybe £48.'

'What! – for a dress. What's the material made of?'

'I really haven't a clue, but it *feels* quite nice.'

'Yes. It does doesn't it. But I can't wear red anyway – it doesn't suit my complexion. Have they got it in any other colours?'

I couldn't be bothered to look so said 'No' and suggested we move on to another store where the clothes were cheaper.

And so the day would drag on until I was fit to drop. We would then sink down in the nearest café for a coffee and a rest, and she would tell me how good I was to take her shopping.

On one of our last visits to Hereford she announced she wanted to go to Chave & Jackson. She compensated for being almost blind by having a phenomenal memory, and although I didn't know where this shop was, when I told her where we were standing, she was able to give me precise instructions and we got to the shop without any difficulty.

'Now,' she said, 'I want the Ester Lauder counter.'

'We're standing in front of it Dolly.'

'Can I help you, madam?' said the assistant.

'Yes,' said Dolly. 'Do you sell White Linen body spray?'

The assistants' eyes lit up as she said, 'Yes madam, would you like a large or medium size?'

'Do you have a sample I can try?'

The assistant came round to the front of the counter and handed her a sample.

'Dolly liberally sprayed it all over herself then, with a disarming smile said, 'Thank you, that's better - I forgot to put mine on this morning.'

To ease my embarrassment and the disappointment of the sales assistant I felt obliged to make a purchase which I didn't really want.

In the July of 2012 Dolly organised a dinner party for several of her friends at a local restaurant. When I asked her what was the occasion she said it was to celebrate her 100th birthday. 'But it's not your birthday until December 25th' I said.

'Yes, but I might not live until then,' she said, 'so I'm celebrating it now.'

She did reach her 100th birthday but died some months later, still taking a pride in her appearance and making her weekly visit to the hairdresser.

FIRST IMPRESSIONS OF HAY

I first visited Hay in the Spring of 1977 when I came to stay with a friend living in a farm cottage at Clyro. At that time, I thought I couldn't live without my weekly fix of Sunday Papers, so when I asked where I could get a newspaper, she looked at me slightly askance, then added after a moments thought, 'The only place you'll get a Sunday Paper here is from a serving hatch at the back of The Swan Hotel in Hay.

Driving along the winding, undulating road from Clyro to Hay, I was immediately struck by the incredibly beautiful scenery surrounding the area, with Hay nestling in the middle of it. Picking my way to The Swan, I passed a huddle of charming stone built houses, and after buying my newspaper, made a leisurely investigation of the town. I looked again at the little row of cottages that I'd noticed on my way in. The end one in particular caught my eye. It was approached by a few steps up from the pavement with an uncared for front garden and a mass of ivy and rose bushes covering the frontage. I fell instantly in love with the place and told myself, unrealistically, that one day I would live there. On reaching the centre of the town, I could confirm that my friend's advice on the only place I would get a newspaper was not misplaced, for there was not a shop, nor pub or a café open and the whole place was uncannily quiet and deserted. Although small, the geography of the town was difficult to figure, especially for someone with a hopeless sense of direction such as I have, and it seemed to have been created haphazardly, without logic or reason, which somehow, only added to the charm of the place.

On a subsequent week-day visit, I noticed there were no prohibitive yellow lines to be seen anywhere and one could park with impunity anywhere there happened to be a space. I remember on one occasion, standing on the pavement in High Town and, along with a few other people, watched a lorry driver trying to extricate himself from where he had parked to make a delivery. The lorry had about a foot or two to spare at the front and the same at the back. If it moved at too much of an angle in one direction it was in danger of knocking a shop sign down and too much in another and it would have been into a shop window, not to mention the possibility of hitting one of the cars parked either end of it. With a great deal of skill and patience, and shouts of advice from the onlookers, the lorry eventually got away without damage to itself or the many obstacles in its way. A person who had been standing next to me on the pavement turned, and with a mischievous smile and the trace of a Welsh accent said, 'Well, that's the most *exciting* thing that's happened *yer* in *yers.!*

Things gradually began to change in this surrealistic, unsophisticated little town, which was due in no small measure to Richard Booth transforming it into the largest second-hand bookshop in the world. The place received a further injection of fame or notoriety (depending on which side of the fence you're sitting) when he bought the castle, declared Home Rule for Hay, appointed himself King Richard, and bestowed the fake title of Duchess of Hay on the world renowned transsexual, April Ashley, who was one of the more colourful residents of Hay at that time. All very much 'tongue in cheek' stuff, but it certainly helped to put Hay on the map. As did the inception in 1988 of the Hay Festival of Literature, the brain child of actor Norman Florence, his wife – actress Rhoda Lewis and their son Peter.Florence, the popularity of which has grown with each year and is now visited by people from all over the world.

They first painted yellow lines in the streets of Hay in about 1978 and then a Traffic Warden started prowling the streets once a week, but one could never be certain on which day this would be. I remember an occasion when a friend of mine was standing in Field's, the greengrocers, waiting to be served, when suddenly, Mr. Field seized a sack of potatoes, asked my friend for the key to her car, opened the boot and dumped the sack in the back. Puzzled, she went outside to protest that she didn't want a sack of potatoes, only to find Mr. Field explaining to the Traffic Warden that she was only parked on the yellow lines long enough for him to load her car. Grateful and deeply impressed with his quick thinking, she drove off, returning later to give back the sack of potatoes and purchase some more fruit and vegetables, which she thought was the very least she could do.

About this time there was a shop in Hay, where the Red Cross Shop now stands. It masqueraded as an antique shop, but, as I recall, there were mostly only bales of hay in the window, and I wondered vaguely how they could make a living with so little to display. I didn't have to wonder for long as subsequently the owners of the premises were arrested for printing illegal bank notes in the cellar.

There was a further bit of excitement when a mentally disturbed gunman held some members of the public hostage for several hours at the old dental surgery. The siege went on for most of the night and only ended when a brave lady seized the gun whilst the man dozed briefly. He was duly arrested, but it was a bit of an anticlimax when it was discovered that the pistol he had been menacingly brandishing was really only a toy replica.

Then of course, in the 1970s Hay was invaded by the so-called New Age Travellers, who obviously knew a good thing when they saw it. They fetched up on the Black Mountains with their tents and a motley assortment of old lorries and caravans and made frequent forays into Hay to get supplies for their frugal needs. They offended many of the respectable inhabitants of Hay, with their straggly beards, long, greasy, unwashed hair, dirty clothing and generally unkempt appearance. Yet many of them came from good family backgrounds and had even given up good careers, to lead, what they imagined would be an alternative, idyllic, carefree lifestyle, where I suspect happiness didn't depend so much on money or possessions, but probably more in the eating of the magic mushrooms that grew in abundance on the slopes and were said to make people laugh manically at the silliest things.

I knew of one person who lived in Hay who was the mother of one of the hippies. She would lodge a sum of money with the local butcher to ensure that her son and some of his fellow travellers could get a good weekly supply of meat. Some of these 'travellers' eventually took up employment in and around Hay and became respectable members of the community, whilst others disappeared as mysteriously as they had come, until all eventually fizzled into obscurity, leaving the sheep and wild ponies to resume their peaceful, untrammelled grazing on the sloping pastures of the Gospel Pass.

Some years after retiring, I moved from my home in Leamington Spa to Hay and, by the magic of serendipity, managed to rent the cottage in Swan Bank that I'd fallen in love with all those years previously. Inside was every bit as charming, quaint and old-fashioned as I'd imagined, with beams on the low ceilings and an ancient, coal-fired, black-leaded grate, in the kitchen/dining area, with ovens either side. There was a charming open fireplace in the living room and the stairs from this room led up to two bedrooms on one side of the cottage, whilst an independent stairway from the dining room led up to another bedroom. I spent five happy years in this house, before the company from whom I rented the property decided to sell and I was obliged to move. Now, I am living in a Harley Almshouse and despite the many changes that have taken place in Hay since my first visit, and the fact that it has now become one of the most visited places in Wales, for me the town has still retained its magic, charm and uniqueness and I feel, in the evening of my life, that I've come home at last.

PUTTING THE FOOT IN MOUTH

It was the spring of 2001 and foot and mouth disease was raging throughout the country. I was sitting in the hairdressers and the conversation centred on the Foot and Mouth crisis and what a disastrous effect it was having on tourism, especially in our little town, which relies heavily on tourists for survival. We all nodded in sympathetic agreement, then, without any break in the chatter, Sally – the hairdresser said, 'Yes, and to make matters worse, did you hear about the ewes that went wild round the town last night and smashed several windows?'

'Really!' I said incredulously. 'Do they know whom they belong to?'

'I don't think so,' said Sally, 'there were about twenty of them altogether.'

'Did the police manage to round them all up and corral them?'

'No', replied Sally, as she studiously mixed the colour for my hair. 'But the police seem to think they're local.' Realising by this time that this conversation didn't quite make sense, I said, 'Well how did they manage to break the windows – did they butt them with their heads?'

'No,' said Sally witheringly, 'the police think they must have used hammers.'

The vision of twenty sheep rampaging through the town wielding hammers and smashing shop windows stretched my credulity to the limit and I said, 'Oh, come on, this is a wind up isn't it. 'Slapping the colour on my hair she said, 'No, honestly, it isn't. Walk up town when you leave here and see for yourself.'

Still puzzled, I began to suspect we must be talking at cross purposes, but added, in a concerned tone, 'The farmer whose sheep they were must be very worried.'

'Who's talking about sheep?' chirped up one of the clients.

'Sally is,' I said. 'Didn't you hear her say about the ewes rampaging through town last night, smashing shop windows?'

Everyone turned to me with a bemused look, then burst into laughter as Sally explained: they weren't *ewes* on the rampage but *youths!*

'Oh,' I said, rather *sheepishly.* 'And did the police catch the culprits?'

'I don't think so, not yet,' said one of the clients.

'If they haven't been caught how do they know there were twenty of them. Fancy twenty youths all going mad in a little town like Hay?'

I finally got the story right. It appeared that *two youths* had rampaged through the town in the night and smashed *twenty* windows.

I really will have to think about getting a hearing aid.

COLD CALLERS

I'd dozed off in the chair and was brought back to consciousness by the ringing of the phone. It was a number I didn't recognise and when I picked it up there was a   long pause, so I said, 'Hello – who is this calling?'

Someone at the other end mumbled something I couldn't catch, so I said, 'I'm sorry – who did you say you were?'

The unknown voice on the other end mumbled something again, which I again failed to grasp, so this time I said irritably, 'Can you please speak slowly and distinctly – I still don't know who you are.'

'This is the Hidden Hearing,' the voice said more loudly. 'We will be in your district for the next few weeks. If you have a problem would you like to make an appointment to have your ears tested?'

'No thank you,' I said. Then added indignantly before replacing the receiver, 'There's nothing wrong with *my* hearing!'

It didn't occur to me until afterwards that the gist of the conversation might well have indicated otherwise.

COLD CALLERS OF ANOTHER KIND

I was on a visit to my great niece who was divorced with one young child. However, her ex-husband's parents still liked to keep in touch and visit their grandson from time to time. On this particular day they had arranged to call at a given time but Katie (great niece) had to pop out for a short while so asked me, if they called before she got back, to look after them.

Presently, the door bell rang and I went to answer it. There stood the grandparents, whom I'd only met briefly before. I welcomed them in, sat them down, explained Katie would be back soon and asked if they'd like a cup of tea. They looked a little bit surprised but after slight hesitation accepted my offer. I put the tea before them, then went into the garden to call in their grandson. He came running in and bounced straight onto the lap of his grandmother. I don't know who was the more startled – she – or the little boy, who leapt off her lap in horror. Before I had time to sort out what was going on, the door bell rang again.

I rushed to answer it and there stood the proper grandparents. I ushered them in and took the other couple into another room, apologising profusely as I did so, while they explained who they were. Feeling a bit silly, I thought the least I could do was

let them finish their tea and give them time to tell me about
God and the way to salvation.

I didn't really think I needed saving – unless it was from my
own stupidity!

THE 'WEIGHS' OF ALL FLESH

Many years after I'd left the bed-sit I'd rented in the home of
Mrs. Moss - my ferocious landlady - I saw her in the local
grocer's shop with her eccentric, middle-aged daughter.

I looked up at her and said, deferentially, 'Hello Mrs.
Moss.'

'Who are *you*?' she said haughtily, as she looked down at me
from her great height.

'I'm Miss Trowbridge,' I said, 'who used to rent a bed-sit
from you.'

'Well you *have* got stout,' she said. Then compounded her
statement by repeating loudly,

'Well!' I wouldn't have recognised you – you *have* got
stout.'

I cringed with embarrassment as other people in the shop spun
round to look at this person who'd got *stout*. It did nothing to
relieve my discomfort when her daughter said, (presumably in

my defence) 'Well mother, she can't look like a little boy *all* her life.'

Needless to say, I slunk out of the shop without waiting to be served. When I got home, in view of my remark-worthy stoutness, I decided, as a reluctant concession to slimming, to forego a proper meal and make do with a biscuit and a cup of tea. The next morning, I stood, starkers, on the bathroom scales and discovered, to my horror, that I'd shot up to 8 stone 7 pounds! How I wish that was all I weighed now.

EMBARRASSING PARTIES

It was my 50th birthday and my friends thought I should do something special. Having accepted the hospitality of many of them in the past, I felt the least I could do would be to book a room at a local hotel and throw a party and invite all my friends and their appendages to come along and celebrate The party was going with a swing and everyone seemed to be enjoying themselves except for one, middle-aged man, whom I didn't know, who was standing by the door looking slightly drunk and miserable as sin.

Because it was my party and I felt it was my duty to make sure everyone was happy, after a while I went over to speak with him and offer him something to eat. He waved the plate of food away with the back of his hand, but despite his rudeness, I persevered and asked him if he would like to dance.

'No,' he said rudely, then added, 'and if I did it would be with someone much younger and prettier than you.'

'In that case Sir,' I said evenly, 'you are obviously at the wrong party, for you won't find anyone younger or prettier than me here, so would you please leave?'

He didn't leave, until a couple of friends propelled him, mildly protesting, out of the door and told him to go and find a party where the ladies would be much more to his taste.

I never did find out who he was or what he was doing at my party in the first place.

* * * * * *

I don't know why I allow myself to be talked into these things, for if I'm truthful, I find throwing, or attending parties almost always gives me more perturbation than pleasure.

On this occasion I was getting a lot of unwanted attention from a terribly boring person whom I hardly knew, and didn't particularly want to know, but from whom I didn't quite know how to extricate myself without seeming to be rude. So when he drifted off to get me a drink, which I didn't really want, I took the opportunity of burying myself in a circle of people and hid behind the tallest person in the hope that I wouldn't be seen.

Tallest person moved, there was no hiding place and I was spotted. Boring bearer of drinks came lurching towards me and in my embarrassment, I foolishly blurted, 'Oh, *there* I am!

THE PENSIONERS PARTY
(circa 2003)

My friend Dolly, in her nineties and partially sighted, asked me to accompany her to a Christmas Party organised for local pensioners. I declined, explaining that it wasn't really my *thing*. She was disappointed and said she wouldn't be able to go if I didn't accompany her, so I relented.

'Oh good,' she said. 'The food was lovely last year and we got some entertainment and I think a lady sang *The Old Rugged Cross* – or was that the year before? I know she's sung it ever such a lot of times. And we get a free raffle ticket and everybody gets a prize,' she enthused. 'I got a lovely hat and scarf to match last year, which I think came from Monica's and I gave it to my niece for Christmas. It was ever so nice.'

'Oh good,' I said. 'Another Christmas present wouldn't come amiss.'

The day of the party arrived and after I'd seen all my Dial-a-Ride passengers safely off the bus, I followed them in. As we entered, each person was asked, in that well meaning, though patronising tone reserved for the elderly, 'Would you like a sherry or mulled wine, dear?'

I opted for the mulled wine, then squeezed into the place reserved for me by Dolly. On the otherwise bare table was a bowl of peanuts and another bowl that *had* contained crisps, but which was now empty save for a few crumbled bits.

I sipped my wine, and in an attempt to be sociable, looked at the lady opposite. She had a paper hat stuck on her head, daringly slanting at a rakish angle, which was totally at variance with her otherwise gloomy countenance. I smiled and tried to engage her in conversation, but she remained glum and uncommunicative, more interested in ramming handfuls of peanuts into her mouth. I stretched out my hand to help myself to a few but quickly withdrew it when said lady was suddenly seized by a fit of sneezing, spraying mucous and half eaten peanuts all over the table.

Dolly, who was not only partially sighted but a bit deaf as well, asked me to pass her the peanuts. 'They've all gone,' I lied.

'Why the greedy bugger!' she hissed. 'She ate nearly all them crisps as well!'

I smiled at nut-stuffing lady again to make her think I didn't mind about the sneezing, but she continued to stare back glumly, the while she stoically persisted in stuffing the nuts.

Then a helper came to the table bearing more wine and sherry and I had another glass of wine to help me feel as if I was enjoying myself – even if I wasn't. It didn't.

I glanced at my watch. One hour gone – two more to go. God spare me!

I looked across at the Mayor, who was standing importantly in the middle of the room, resplendent in his robes of office and flowing grey beard. I half smiled, but he stared back vacantly. No cheer there then.

A highly intelligent lady to my right told me she could speak over thirty different languages, including Welsh. Since the only language I could lay my tongue to was English I was enormously impressed.

Feeling hungry and wondering if the crisps and nuts (of which I'd had none) were all we were going to get, I was pleased when, at last, the kind helpers appeared with trays of sandwiches, sausage rolls, quiches etcetera. We all helped ourselves to polite portions with the exception of the nut-eater who, I was intrigued to observe, would grab a sandwich, or a piece of quiche, sausage roll or whatever, take a bite out of it, then discard the remains, until her plate was piled high with revolting lumps of rejected food.

Time for the entertainment and those with their backs to the entertainers turned their chairs the better to see. Mrs. Glum Nut-Eater turned her chair and unconsciously planted her right elbow plum in the middle of her partially eaten food, and there it remained throughout the whole of the entertainment, for she never clapped once.

Someone played the piano with more enthusiasm than skill and some children came to sing carols and old fashioned songs such as *Daisy, Daisy* and *Pack up Your Troubles* and we were encouraged to join in. At least no one came to sing *The Old Rugged Cross* which was a relief.

I found it more interesting watching the people than listening to, or joining in with the singing and one lady in particular, diagonally across the room from me caught, my attention. She sat, shoulders hunched, legs crossed and arms folded over her ample bosom. Her head drooped and her eyes were closed as if in sleep, but each time the audience clapped, she raised her head, yawned expansively, clapped feebly, then promptly dropped off again.

Entertainment over, it was now time for the raffle. The Mayor stood behind a huge table which groaned with prizes and in the light of what Dolly had told me, I looked forward to the calling of my ticket number. It took ages for all the numbers to be called and the lucky people to struggle up to the table to select their prizes. Finally, it was all over and I swear I must have been the only one in the room not to get a raffle prize. I'd endured all this and not even a prize to make it worthwhile.

It was the first and last OAP's Christmas Party I ever attended, having decided I wasn't really suited to being old anyway.

THE IMPROBABLE THINGS WE BELIEVE

At a small gathering of mostly older people, we began to amuse ourselves by relating things we believed to be true when we were very young, but which we realised were not so when we reached the age of discernment.

I recalled being told by my mother to be careful when licking my ice cream cornet. If I dropped it, she warned, and it landed on my toes, it would smash them to pieces. I believed it for a while and always licked with great care, until one day I dared myself to accidentally on purpose drop the cornet on my feet to see what would *really* happen.

I gave an involuntary, frightened yell as it landed, but was then relieved to find that, although my shoes and the floor were a sticky mess, my toes hadn't been smashed and they didn't even hurt.

I'VE GOT MY BEADY EYE ON YOU

The story that amused me most was related by Elizabeth, our hostess. She said that when they were small children her grandmother looked after them whilst her parents were at work.

Granny had a glass eye and if she had to leave them alone for any reason she would remove her eye and place it in a prominent position on the high mantelshelf, then warn them:

Don't any of you misbehave whilst I'm gone. I shall know if you do because I shall be keeping my eye on you.

SO NOW WE KNOW

A friend, who was about seven at the time, overheard an adult conversation about a neighbour who already had seven children and was about to give birth to her eighth.

'Huh,' said one of them. 'She's only got to look at a pair of men's underpants and she's pregnant.

Shortly after my friend was on a train journey. The train slowed up as it reached its destination and she was alarmed to see rows of men's underpants wafting in the breeze on a back garden clothes-line.

Her mother just couldn't understand why she suddenly clasped her hands over her eyes and wouldn't remove them until the journey was over.

NIGHTIME TERRORS

Lions and tigers prowled my bedroom at night and ghosts lurked in the shadows cast by a candle. Come daylight, they all magically faded away.

If I had to go upstairs in the dark for any reason, although neither seen nor heard, I knew the ghosts were there waiting to get me. In my fear of the unknown I became fearless in my flight from it and remember at least one occasion when I leapt from the top of the stairs to the bottom, convinced I was being pursued by a ghostly presence.

I rushed into the kitchen, where most winter evenings were spent, and flew into the unsuspecting lap of my mother.

'Why are you so frightened?' she asked.

'The ghosts,' I murmured.

'Don't be silly,' she said. 'There are no such things as ghosts.'

'Oh yes there are!' I countered. 'What about The Holy Ghost?'

Note: I am pleased to see that in the modern *Book of Common Prayer* there is no longer a *Holy Ghost* but a much less frightening presence - *The Holy Spirit.*

OH NO! A HOLIDAY IN ACCRINGTON?

Now that I am so very old I no longer have the desire to spread my wings abroad for a holiday, especially when I realise how much of the British Isles are left unvisited by me. So I was pleased when a friend asked me to accompany her on a coaching holiday somewhere up North, especially when some of the scheduled excursions included travel by rail.

The coach picked us up in Brecon on the Monday morning, but when I looked at the itinerary my friend handed me after we'd settled into our seats, I felt just a little disappointed, as it stated that the hotel originally featured in the brochure was incorrect and that we would now be staying at an hotel in Accrington.

Who, in their right mind, would want to spend five days at an Hotel in Accrington, I thought, a place which, if I thought about it at all, I'd always understood to be a grim, northern, heavily industrialised town, with grime laden houses and Lowry match stick men peopling the drab streets. And indeed, it may well have been as I imagined, but I would never know for we didn't actually get to see the town, for the hotel we were taken to was situated in the country a few miles outside Accrington; a huge, grand, castellated edifice which stood in seventeen acres of wooded parkland, with many of the trees splendidly clad in all their autumnal glory. After such a long journey, it was a real pleasure to be shown to our spacious, tastefully furnished, twin-bedded room overlooking the park.

I didn't like the bathroom much though. It was no friend to me, for although it was large and bristling with cleanliness and chrome and contained all the little extras one expects to find in a luxury Four Star Hotel, the lighting was much too bright and revealing. There were too many large mirrors, none of which spared me and I could see myself getting *into* the bath, whilst I was *in* the bath and getting *out* of the bath, and what I saw did not please me, but I could not avert my eyes as the hateful, all revealing mirrors lined the walls.

The unwelcome sight of all my flabbiness did not, however, deter me from enjoying a pre-prandial drink in one of the many beautifully furnished lounges, before tucking in to a three course meal in the elegant dining room. During the meal, I introduced myself and Jackie to our nearest sitters at the dining table and learned that the gentleman and his wife to my left were called Derek and Betty, that they came from Tavistock, had both served in the navy during the war, and that he was in remission from prostate cancer and his wife was recovering from a stroke. So she and Jackie had an illness in common, although I could scarcely claim to have anything in common with Derek's complaint.

The two elderly ladies on my right were twin sisters named Joan and Joyce. Joan was a widow and Joyce had left her husband behind, complaining he never wanted to go anywhere. They looked exactly alike and both spoke with a most agreeable Gloucestershire accent. They ordered the same food for each course and both left exactly the same amount of uneaten food on their plates, and I was fascinated to see they did the same thing at every evening meal throughout their stay.

After a good night's sleep, we were up early the next morning and had a *Full English* before starting out at 8.30 am for the first of our daily excursions. The day did not look promising as a heavy mist hung in the damp air, and as we were being taken on a scenic journey, I reflected there was not going to be much scenery to be seen. I need not have worried, for in less than half an hour, the mist cleared and we were able to see and fully appreciate the spectacular beauty of the vast stretches of moorland and heather clad hills in all their sunlit splendour.

I noticed a lot of curious looking coloured sheep dotted about the landscape and learned from our very informative driver that they were known as Herdwick sheep and that they had three changes of colour during their life time. They were born black, but after a few months turned brown and should they be lucky enough to survive lambhood and become ewes, they then turned grey with a hint of red. It seems the reason this breed flourishes in the Lake District is because, after Beatrix Potter became rich as a result of her books, she bought several farms to add to the one she already worked, and tenanted the rest out to other farmers. But one of the conditions of letting was that the tenants must agree to breed these unique sheep and after she died, her Will stipulated that this rule must apply in perpetuity.

I was interested to learn that she had started writing quite by accident. It is well known that she did not like children and had none of her own. However, she did have a godson who was a sickly child and during one of his illnesses she felt it her duty to write to him. So she wrote: *I haven't got any news to tell you and don't know what to say to you so I'll tell you a story instead.*

She then wrote and illustrated a story and he so enjoyed it that his parents encouraged her to write more stories and the rest is history.

We reached Settle on the coach, where we alighted at the railway station to catch a train to take us to Carlisle on

England's most scenic railway, passing through Kirby Stephen, Appleby (of Horse Fair fame), the Eden Valley and over the impressive twenty-four arched Ribblehead viaduct – sometimes featured in T.V. programmes.

I was impressed with how beautifully the station at Settle and subsequent stations were looked after. They were just as I remembered small railway stations from early childhood, clean and pleasant and liberally be-hung with baskets of carefully tended, freshly blooming begonias, busy lizzies, brachycome and lobelia. On enquiring, I learned that these stations were lovingly cared for by volunteer railway enthusiasts.

Our journey ended at Carlisle's Citadel Station, which nestled confidently against the impressive red city walls. We had two hours to explore the town and have a light lunch before our coach took us on another journey, this time into part of the Lake District, through Ullswater and on to Windermere, where we had a short stop for a look around and a cup of tea. Then it was onto the coach again to take us back to the Hotel, via the famously tortuous, though spectacularly beautiful Kirkstone Pass.

The following morning, the weather again looked unpromising, having rained heavily all night, but we were not going to let that deter us, and yet again, within a short space of time, the rain stopped and the whole countryside was once more bathed in sunshine.

This time, the coach took us along the steeply undulating, arduous stretches of the beautiful Pendle Trail, so called because this was the trail the famous Pendle Witches had to walk on their way to Lancaster Castle, to face trial as witches. There were ten men and women in all, and all were convicted largely on the evidence of an eight year old girl, known locally as Squinting Lizzie. Twenty one years later, she herself was accused of being a witch and was hanged. It seems the purge of the witches began when an old woman asked a peddler for some pins. He said he would let her have some if she had the money to pay, but she had none, so he refused her the pins.

Shortly after he had a sudden illness which rendered him paralysed and unable to speak, and it was thought to have been caused by the old woman casting a wicked spell on him.

I could not help but feel sorry for these poor wretches, who'd had to walk for three days to come before the trial judge, whom they knew would sentence them to death. I wondered what, if anything, they'd had to eat on the way; where they laid their heads at night and whether they had tried to comfort one another on their journey, or squabbled amongst themselves and accused each other of treachery, or whether they walked in fearful silence. It seems two of the accused ladies were eighty years old and one of them, Mrs. Demdyke, died in prison before she came to trial.

They were probably not witches anyway, but people who tried to cure illnesses by the use of potions made from various plants. So I suppose, if someone did not recover after imbibing one of the potions, the person administering the cure could be thought to be a murdering witch. If they'd lived in this day and age they could well have been thought of as highly respected homeopaths. When we reached Lancaster, I looked up at the castle where they'd been tried and hanged and felt an overwhelming sense of sadness.

It was Market Day in Lancaster and we wandered around briefly looking at the many colourful, interesting stalls, and although I would have liked to explore this interesting town further, walking was not easy for my friend so we opted for a café and a sit down until it was time to get on the move on again.

The coach took us back to the Hotel via Morecombe Bay, a place with which I was singularly unimpressed. The tide was out and there were endless stretches of flat, dirty mud stretching for what seemed like miles. Our all-knowing coach driver pointed out the place where the ill-fated Chinese cockle pickers had met their death, when they were trapped by the incoming tide. We were told that when the tide *does* come in, it is with a great rush, faster than a man could run. I would have liked to have seen it.

The next day, our coach took us through yet more scenic countryside to the railway station at Carnforth, where we had an hour or more to spend before boarding another train. This was the station where the story Brief Encounter was filmed with Celia Johnson and Trevor Howard in the leading parts. For some years, this station had fallen into dereliction, until some railway enthusiasts, businesses and the Town Council all got together to renovate it. Now, it is an absolute delight, the buffet room having been restored to exactly as it was at the time of filming, even to the old fashioned heavy manual till on the counter. The Waiting Room was clean and pleasant and to add a touch of authenticity, they'd even piled up old fashioned leather luggage cases and small attaché cases on a trolley in a corner.

The volunteer railway staff were smiling and helpful and told me that during the holiday season, a couple would come in dressed in clothes similar to those worn by Celia Johnson and Trevor Howard in the film and would sit in the buffet near the window, gazing lovingly at each other until the train came in, when they would tearfully part in a cloud of steam.

In what might have once been the station master's office, there was a television which showed the black and white film – Brief Encounter – all day every day, but as it lasts over eighty minutes, there was no chance of us being able to watch it.

On the walls of the waiting area, stuck between the lovely old pictures one used to see in railway waiting rooms in the olden days, were reminiscences by local people of how things were during the war. The ladies of the W.V.S. used to serve the troops, many of whom passed through the station, with jam jars of unsweetened tea and sandwiches made with powdered egg. I was intrigued when a lady from our party said she well remembered it, but used to feel very aggrieved because they would not serve her with any tea or sandwiches as she was in the Land Army and that didn't count as being in the forces.

I wished we'd had more than an hour to spend at this delightful station but our train came all too soon to take us on another interesting journey, ending at Barrow-in-Furness. We travelled through some beautiful countryside, but a lot of the time the railway took us over vast stretches of salt flats, where there was not a lot to see except more and more salt flats. Surprisingly, sheep grazed these flats and it is said that they have a most distinct and pleasant flavour when cooked. Aside from the sheep, I saw five herons and two cormorants and numerous other, smaller birds wading at the edge of the tide, which I could not identify. At times we seemed to be travelling on low aqueducts with a calm sea surrounding us on all sides.

Eventually we reached Barrow-in-Furness, now transferred from Lancashire to Cumbria. Pulling into the station, the approach epitomised everything I'd ever thought about grim, dirty, industrialised northern towns and for a moment or two I thought: what on earth are we going to do in a dump like this. Then I remembered the coach was going to meet us at the station and there indeed it was, waiting to take us on yet another scenic route back to Grange-over-Sands, which was one of the stations we'd passed through.

On arrival, the coach driver told us there was a very good Tea Room called The Hazlemere which had won an award for being the best Tea Room in Britain and he could recommend it. It wasn't far from the car park and Jackie and I made straight for it and were not disappointed. There was a wonderful array of fancy cakes and pastries to delight the eye and palette and all sorts of exotic biscuits and jams and tempting goodies, but bearing in mind the vision I had of myself in the brightly mirrored bathroom and the fact that I would later be eating a three course meal, I restricted myself to a virtuous chicken salad and took my pleasure in watching Jackie gorge on the cakes.

The journey back to the Hotel would, I understand, have been yet another scenic delight, but we did not see much of it as a heavy mist had descended, but it had nevetheless been a wonderful day's excursion.

Friday was our last day and we were scheduled to travel back after breakfast. Whilst sitting in one of the lounges killing a bit of time before the coach came, I happened to look up at the ceiling and was amazed to see how incredibly beautiful it was. There were intricate patterns in red and raised gold all round the edges of the room, and in the centre hung a gold chandelier with several candle-shaped bulbs. I was still gazing up in wonder when a fairly elderly gentleman, who was obviously something to do with the Hotel, for he wore a badge, came by. I remarked to him about the wonderful ceiling and spent the next half hour or so being told all about the Dunkenhalgh Hotel. It was over seven hundred years old, having initially been built as a monastery in 1285 but with the dissolution of the monasteries, it was eventually bought by the Rishtons as a private residence, which family held it for nearly two hundred and fifty years, after which it was sold, in 1571 to

Thomas Walmesley, an eminent judge, popularly known as the hanging judge, because of the frequency with which he condemned people to be hanged for what would now be considered fairly trivial crimes.

After the death in 1642 of Sir Thomas Walmesley the estate was passed to his grandson Richard. The following year the house was occupied by Roundhead soldiers the night before the battle of Whalley.

The Dunkenhalgh estate passed from the Walmesleys to the Petres by the marriage in 1712 of Catherine Walmesley to Robert 7th Lord Petre, who died the following year leaving Catherine, aged sixteen years, a widow with a baby son.

In the following year, the greater part of the house, largely ruinous, was pulled down and rebuilt in its present, castellated gothic style, but it is probable that some of the internal walls and foundations are original.

Robert, my informant, told me that he had worked at the Dunkenhalgh Hotel for over forty years, that he had written two books about the place and that he loved it dearly. He added that during the war it had been taken over by the army for the training of army officers, but that the then owners would only allow this, provided that all the ceilings and walls were boarded up to preserve and protect them.

He then took me into rooms that normally the public did not have admission to. One of them was known as the Oak Room, which had the most amazing oak panelling throughout, including the ceiling. This panelling had, apparently, in the early eighteenth century, been misappropriated from Hacking Hall, another house on the estate.

The next room he took me into was known as the Portrait Room and there hung some splendid portraits of members of families past, including one of Judge Walmesley, whom I thought looked like evil personified.

There was also a portrait of a very beautiful lady, whose eyes, I was told, followed you wherever you went. I walked all round the room and found this to be true. He told me she had come from a good family in France to be a governess to the Petre family children. She was seduced by the promise of marriage by an English army officer, who, when he realised she was pregnant, deserted her. Not wishing to return to her family in France and there being no future for her at the Dunkenhalgh, she took her own life by throwing herself off the bridge into the rushing torrents. Later, her brother challenged her seducer to a duel and killed him, thus avenging the untimely death of his beautiful sister. Her ghost is still said to haunt the place.

All too soon, the coach arrived to take us home, thus ending abruptly my fascinating conversation with this most pleasant and informative gentleman, who had really put the icing on the cake to what had been a most enjoyable few days holiday.

RANTS ABOUT ANTS

Of all the creatures and insects that inhabit our world, I think ants must figure high on my list of pet hates. I murder without mercy the hateful little hordes that invade my kitchen each year, even though I go to extraordinary lengths to discourage them, even making sure there is nothing left lying around which would encourage them to invade my space. But come the summer, they still arrive with relentless regularity.

Ant powder seems not to deter them; rivers of undiluted bleach liberally spread over the stone doorstep does not stop them from brazenly marching in, and pouring kettles of boiling water over the ground where I think their nests might be has no effect. I seal up cracks in the window frames and block off air vents and even put masking tape round holes where electric wires come through, but the tenacious, persistent little critters still find a way in.

They race over the draining board, creep over the top of the cooker, crawl up the wall to the shelf where I keep my jars of coffee, sugar and rice, and I'm left wondering what attraction there is up there for them. I soon find out. Taking the sugar jar down, I discover that although the lid is firmly on and sealed with a rubber band, small remnants of sugar have gathered round the rim and the ants are having a banquet. I remove the lid and find they have somehow managed to wriggle into the jar. I slay the ants and throw the sugar on the compost heap and hope that the ants that have escaped death at my hands will eventually find their way over there and leave me alone; but not a bit of it. Back they come the next day and I can only conclude that the previous occupant of this property might have been a little more generous spirited towards them and they're working on inherited memory.

I have read that, although small, ants are highly intelligent and resourceful. If this is true, and I've no way of disproving it, why haven't they enough intelligence to tell their mates, 'Don't go there – you won't find much to eat and you'll most likely get killed!'

This leads me to think that perhaps they don't come of their own free will, but are ordered, by a higher authority in the ant world to go on their raids. Much like, I imagine, a high ranking army officer, safely ensconced in his headquarters, might order his troops into battle, aware that lives have to be sacrificed for the ultimate good of their country. In the case of ants, I suppose they die in unquestioning service for the greater good of their colony.

In the overall scheme of things, I suppose the number of ants slain by me is miniscule, for according to researcher – Nigel Franks – ants outnumber human beings by some two hundred million to one and the combined weight of ants throughout the world is allegedly greater than that of human beings.

It is said that ants have colonised every land mass on Earth and thrive in deserts, jungles, swamps and tundra, not forgetting of course, my back kitchen. So it seems, that if I want to live in a totally ant-free environment, the only place I will find it is in the frozen polar wastes and on the top of the highest ice-capped mountains.

On balance, I think I'd prefer to live where I am and deal, as best I can with the yearly invasion of these pesky little creatures. And who knows, one day someone might be able to tell me how essential they are to planet earth's ecology. Until then, I shall continue to hate them.

Well – we all need something to hate don't we.

IGNORANCE IS BLISS

Twiddling the knobs on the bedside radio one sleepless night I was amused to hear someone relating the following:

At the end of the second World War there were a lot of bored soldiers kicking their heels in the Middle East anxiously awaiting transportation to take them back home to Britain. As is often the way with soldiers when the fighting is over, there is not much else to do but visit the local bars, get drunk and make a general nuisance of themselves. Something had to be done and the Top Brass, in its infinite wisdom, decided it would be no bad thing to try to introduce a bit of culture into their lives and to this end, arranged to send out lecturers from the U.K. to give them talks on various aspects of the arts.

And so, at morning muster they were accordingly instructed by the sergeant major:

'Now you 'orrible lot, next week we have a very clever man coming all the way from England especially to give you some very interesting talks. I am informed his first talk will be about Keats. Pay close attention and listen to what he has to say and you might learn something.'

As an after thought he then added, 'I doubt if you ignorant lot even know what a 'keat' is.'

With apologies to the unknown narrator on Radio 4

THINGS AREN'T ALWAYS WHAT THEY SEEM

I went out with a few a few friends to celebrate my 80th birthday. Two of the friends were vets and married to each other and during the course of conversation they expressed their admiration that at my age I had recently taken up computing.

There followed some discussion about what make of computer I had, what was my email address, was I using Windows XP and did I have a digital camera etcetera.

I answered all their questions as best I could, but being a bit deaf, I don't always hear what is being said to me, so switched off when the meal came, putting my concentration into the eating of the food.

But I wasn't to be spared and at one point David looked directly at me and said, 'We have a nudist come to the surgery practically every month.'

'*Really!*' I said, incredulously. 'What do you do about it?'

'Nothing usually,' he said, in what I thought an inappropriately laid back attitude.

'What about the people in the waiting room?' I asked. 'How do they react?'

'It doesn't affect them,' he replied, looking mildly puzzled.

I dropped the conversation and turned my attention back to my food, the while I pondered on the monthly visit to the surgery of the naked woman. I wanted to know more, so, a few mouthfuls later, I quietly inquired of his wife, Ros, who was sitting next to my *good* ear,

'What's this about a nudist turning up at the surgery every month then?'

'What nudist,' she exclaimed, her voice loud with astonishment.

'You know,' I said, 'the one that David said comes to the surgery at least once a month.'

They all stopped eating and looked at me as if I'd suddenly lost my marbles.

'That isn't a *nudist,*' Ros guffawed. 'It's a *New Disc!'*

WHEN BLOOD IS THICKER THAN URINE

After a routine blood test, it was discovered that my haemoglobin count was dangerously low and I was whisked off to hospital for blood transfusions. I left hospital feeling very much better than when I went in, so quickly returned to my normal activities, which included singing with a local choral society. We were rehearsing the St. Matthew Passion and were not supposed to talk during rehearsals.

However, whilst the musical director was busy berating the sopranos for being flat, Nelda, the very Welsh lady who always stood next to me whispered, 'How is yew-er bladder now?' Puzzled, I whispered back, 'There's nothing wrong with my bladder.'

'No, yew-er *bladder!*' she repeated.

Feeling a little affronted, I said, 'I've told you, there's nothing wrong with my *bladder.*'

'Well,' she said, 'there might not be anything wrong with yew-er bladder, but your urine's not so good is it?'

'There's nothing wrong with my bladder and nothing wrong with my urine either,' I hissed indignantly.

'Well, there might not be anything wrong with *yew-er bladder* but *yew-er yer-ing's* not so good is it?' she said, touching her ear.

Only then did I realise that it was my *blood* she was enquiring after, not my bladder, and suggesting it was my *hearing* not my *urine* that was fault.

I have, at last, come to the conclusion that I really must get a hearing aid.

OXYMORON STATEMENTS

At the risk of being considered vain, I am prepared to acknowledge that I *do* look a bit younger than my ninety something years and freely admit it is flattering to be reminded of this by people who often ask what is the secret. The truth is that I don't really know, but I sometimes answer with a teasing smile, 'Excessive moderation in all things.

A PEACEFUL SUMMER EVENING

Imagine the scene. Two unmarried, elderly ladies living out the evening of their lives in the cloistered atmosphere of the local almshouses. One sunny summer evening we were sitting on a wooden bench in the garden, sharing a bottle of red wine and discussing, as is the wont of old people, our various ailments and afflictions. When we'd exhausted this inexhaustible subject, I think my friend decided it was time to enliven the conversation by telling me a dirty joke.

Rather than explode with raucous laughter I said, 'I didn't get that - can you tell it to me again?'

She repeated it and I said, 'I still don't get it – say it again?'

Exasperated, she rounded on me and in her irascible Oxford accent, unexpectedly exploded, 'Oh, no wonder you're a f......g virgin!'

At last I was able to laugh and retorted, 'That's a bit of a contradiction in terms isn't it?'

It was time for us both to laugh and have another sip of wine. And I never did get the joke!

ABSENT-MINDED MOMENTS
A VACUUM DELIVERY

I once had a couple of friends who were both midwives and shared a house together. They were sometimes on call for *home* or *emergency* births and on this occasion it was Gwen who was on duty.

The telephone rang in the middle of the night and Gwen tumbled sleepily out of bed to answer it. The call was from an anxious husband whose wife had gone into premature labour.

Gwen hastily got dressed, seized her birthing bag and was just rushing out of the door when her friend, who'd got up to make a cup of tea, called her back and asked, 'What are you going to do Gwen – try and suck it out?'

It was only then that Gwen realised she was making off with the cylinder vacuum cleaner instead of her mid-wife's bag.

HA! THERE YOU ARE

I was on a visit to my sister who lived at a seaside resort in Kent. It was a glorious, hot sunny day and we planned a little shopping, lunch at our favourite restaurant, then an afternoon soaking up the sun on the beach.

I was pleased to find a parking space right outside the very shop I wished to visit, so I happily leapt out of the car and went inside. Having found an article of clothing that I liked, I turned to her for her approval, but she was nowhere to be seen, so I purchased the item without asking her advice, then took the escalator up to another floor in case she'd escaped up there.

Couldn't find her, so I then left the shop and wandered around a few adjacent shops but still no sign, so as the café we'd planned to visit was quite near, I went there in the hope that she might have gone in for a sit down to wait for me. Alas, she wasn't there either, so I made my way back to the car to await her return.

I unlocked the door and was shocked to see her sitting there, in the passenger seat, looking hot, cross and about to expire.

'I've been looking for you everywhere,' I exploded. 'How on earth did you get in when I *know* I locked the car door?'

'I never got out,' she panted, 'you locked me in before I had a chance. I couldn't even open the electric windows to get some air.'

To make amends, I treated her to lunch, but despite this and my humbling apologies, she still found it difficult to forgive my absentmindedness or share in my scarcely concealed amusement. Neither did we sun ourselves on the beach afterwards as planned, as she said she was already too hot and sticky. So we drove home in sulky silence and she didn't cheer up until she'd had a shower and we sat in the garden afterwards, where I tried to make amends by extravagantly admiring her beautiful flower baskets.

MODERN TECHNOLOGY

Of all the miraculous modern inventions I hate the most it has to be mobile phones that take photographs. It doesn't matter where you go or what you do, there's always someone who wants to take a photograph.

I freely admit there are occasions when this facility can be extremely useful, but I do strongly object when, for the flimsiest of reasons, out come the mobiles and you're snapped eating, drinking, talking, or even just sitting innocently trying to be as unobtrusive as possible. They get you every time!

This is invariably followed by the snappers invitation to view their happy snapping and I am *always,* but *always*, simply horrified at how ugly I look - not at all in accordance with my un-snapped vision of myself.

But almost worse than the obligatory peering at oneself on a 2 x 3 inch screen is when the snapper does you the doubtful favour of sending the photos by email. This is all very well for young, beautiful people, but I am an old lady in my nineties, and even when I put on what I think of as my best face; try a smile without showing my teeth, or give a fulsome smile showing my teeth or even just try to look relaxed and happy, the result is always the same. The thinness of my hair is accentuated, every skin blemish and blotch is magnified, the whites of my eyes look red and weary and I never seem to look pleasant or interesting. This has the effect of dropping my self-esteem several notches and I am also of the opinion that all this happy snapping is a personal intrusion into my privacy. Although, to be fair, I might think differently of I was young and a delight to the eye.

As it is, I suppose I shall just have to put up with being constantly reminded how plain and un-photogenic I really am and try to be extra kind and charming to people to make up for my loss of youth and good looks.

WELL I NEVER!

Many years ago, in company with other members of a church I once attended, I went on a religious retreat to a place in North Devon. In between prayers, hymn singing and mild bouts of religiosity, we would walk to the nearest town to do the things tourists usually do – make for the nearest café, have a cup of tea and an indulgent scone with thick cream and jam, then a wander round the shops.

On entering a fancy goods shop the smiling man behind the counter said, 'Hello Lynn, how are you?'

'I'm fine,' I beamed, 'but how d'you know me?'

'I know you well,' he said, 'don't you remember me?'

'No, I'm sorry,' I said, 'I can't really place you. Are you sure you've got the right person?'

'Oh yes,' he said. 'you're Lynn Trowbridge and you come from Leamington Spa. Are you on holiday?'

Bewildered and vaguely embarrassed that I couldn't place him, I bought a few things that I didn't really want, as a sort of compensation for failing to recognise him when he so obviously knew me.

When I joined the others and told them of my encounter with the shopkeeper who knew me but who, for the life of me, I couldn't place, they laughed, as they pointed out that I still had the tag bearing my name and the place I came from pinned to my blouse.

STRANGE ENCOUNTER

After retiring to Hay I worked part-time in a Celtic Craft shop a couple of days a week and loved chatting to the people who came in, especially if they were tourists.

One day a middle-aged gentleman came in with two ladies. They separated to look around and after selecting some merchandise the gentleman came to my desk to pay. But after we completed the transaction and exchanged a few pleasantries he didn't move away as one would have expected but stood in front of my desk just looking at me.

I didn't feel annoyed, uncomfortable or intimidated. On the contrary, I felt an inexplicable affinity and warmth towards him and eventually raised my eyes and boldly said: 'I hope you don't mind my saying so but I *know* I don't know you, yet I feel as if I do.'

'I feel exactly the same way about you,' he said. 'I was drawn to you immediately I walked in the shop.'

We thought we might be unknowingly related but concluded that we weren't. The two ladies he'd entered with came over to pay for their purchases and he introduced them as his wife and mother-in-law. Then after lingering a little longer he said, quite seriously, 'I think we must have known each other in another existence,' then added before leaving, 'I will be back.'

Shortly after the shop closed down and I never saw him again. But I have never forgotten this strange encounter.

BREAKFAST CONVERSATION

'Would you like a boiled egg for breakfast Clare?'

'No thanks.'

'Why not? I'm having one.'

'Because they're fattening and I'm trying to slim.'

'They're not actually.'

'Oh – how d'you work that out?'

'Because it takes more energy to digest a hard boiled egg than the calorific value of the egg.'

'In that case I'll have two.'

OLD AGE

When I was young older people repeated, almost like a mantra: 'It's old age'; 'Anno Domini'; 'I'm not as young as I was', or sometimes distressingly slapping their forehead saying, 'Sorry –I've got a memory like a sieve'.

Looking back, I feel these semi-jocular, oft repeated clichés might well have been an unconscious means of masking the disturbing, insidious signs of ageing and I am frequently reminded of what it entails. Slowness in accomplishing trivial tasks; forgetting words; meeting people and finding it difficult to retrieve their name, or how it is I'm supposed to know them, not to mention being frequently beset by some vague ache or discomfort. Then of course, the invasive questions in the sleepless night. How shall I die? Where? Will I be alone? Will anyone come to my funeral and should I be buried or burned?

Then, entering The Mystery: Will it be hell or heaven or nothingness? In moments of despair – it's hell. In times of optimism – it's heaven, and in times of placidity – nothingness.

But it's spring, the birds will continue to sing, the leaves will keep unfurling beautiful, translucent green leaves, life will renew itself and Nature won't care a damn whether I'm dead or alive.

MY AGEING NEIGHBOUR

My ageing neighbour – Meg – was a lovely person; kind, friendly and generous almost to a fault and with a nice sense of humour. She began her working life as a ballet dancer and in later years became a T.V. producer until she and her husband retired. Now widowed, she had time on her hands, so we sometimes went out for meals together and on one occasion, for a brief holiday.

But age and a love of alcohol began to take their toll on her, impairing her memory and sometimes causing her to speak in a less inhibited way than she might otherwise have done. This could be a bit embarrassing at times, especially as she began to make frequent use of the 'F' word, although it was always delivered in cultured tones. On this particular occasion we were on a brief break staying at a very nice hotel in Montgomeryshire. During the conversation over breakfast she unconsciously used the 'F' word a few times and although I tried to ignore it, I noticed other diners look across at us in astonishment.

So I said, very quietly, 'Meg, will you try not to use the 'F' word?'

'Oh, sorry, sorry,' she protested, 'I didn't realise.'

A little later, out it came again, so once more I whispered, 'Meg – you've said the 'F' word again.'

'Of fuck! so I have', she said, slapping her knee. 'Sorry! Sorry!'

I didn't actually choke on my breakfast but swallowed it down more quickly than was good for my digestion, and did my best to nod and smile graciously as we threaded our way out of the dining room.

MORE THOUGHTS ON AGEING

Now that I am in a very advanced state of elderliness, it is perhaps understandable that it is something that occupies my thoughts from time to time.

On a pessimistic level Anthony Powell writes:
Growing old is like being increasingly penalised for a crime you haven't committed.

On a more optimistic level, I say:
To keep the heart unwrinkled, be hopeful, cheerful, reverent and you will triumph over old age.

ALSO

There are days of oldness, then one gets young again. It goes backward and forward – never in one direction
There is a fountain of youth: it is made manifest in your mind, your talents, the creativity you bring to your life and the lives of other people.

One Liner – Anon.
If you think you are too small to be effective – try going to bed with a mosquito.

COMMUNICATION MADE EASIER - BUT LESS COMMUNICATIVE

We give of ourselves when we speak or write kindly words; give praise to that which is worthy of praise; inspire or encourage flagging endeavour, or give balm to ease the troubled soul. It has been said that the only true gift we can bestow upon others is to give a portion of ourselves.

Yet how often these days do we take time to actually sit down and write a letter. There are printed cards for everything and every occasion and all we have to do is sign them. Or even more impersonal – send an email - oh so very convenient - but how much more exciting and satisfying to have a real letter plop through the letter box.

Only yesterday I received an email from a longstanding friend with all the (now accepted as normal) nauseating abbreviations in common use. Part of it read "Will call u later 2 c how u r" ending: "My luv 2 u" I hated it – and when I reply (by email but unabbreviated) I shall tell him so. It's almost the spoken equivalent of saying: "I can hardly spare you my breath."

I like to move with the times but there *are* limits as to how far I'm prepared to move, and whenever possible I will still cling to the more personal and traditional means of communication. There is nothing more satisfying than the feel of a good pen between ones fingers, penning proper words on pleasing notepaper which one hopes, when posted, will give the recipient as much pleasure as it has given the writer to write it.

AN EVENING IN THE LOCHS & GLENS

Some time ago my friend and I went on a 'Lochs & Glens' coaching holiday to Scotland. We stayed at a very nice Hotel and shared our table with a youngish couple from the Black Country.

He was a tall, quiet man, stoic, with the ravages of constant pain and suffering etched on his otherwise handsome features, whilst his wife was an animated, talkative, slightly scatty red-head, anxious to be friendly and pleasant.

I responded accordingly and introduced my friend saying, 'This is Clare and I'm Lynn, and you are?

She responded, '*Oim* Michelle (spelt the French way) and this is my 'usband – Neil.'

'Nice to meet you both.'

'And *yow.*'

Michelle busied herself with the menu. 'Wot yow 'aving Neil?'

'Don't know – 'aven't seen the menu yet 'ave I.'

'Oim a vegetarian, so Oim going to 'ave the *Mushroon Stroginoff* on a bed of ice. Wot you 'aving Ni-eel?'

'Don't know – 'aven't seen the menu yet.'

'Oh, it's got roast pork 'ere – you like pork don't you Neil.'

The waiter came to take our orders.

'He'll have roast pork and I'll have the Mushroom Stroganoff on a bed of ice.'

Clare and I gave our orders and the food duly arrived. I was intrigued by Michelle's choice and looked across at her plate. Seeing no ICE, I said, 'What was it you ordered Michelle?'

'Mushroon Stroginoff on a bed of ice.'

'I can't actually see any ice,' I said, intrigued, 'but you have got some rice.' She reached over to examine the menu again.

'Oh yes,' she said. 'It's on a bed of rice. I didn't notice the R.'

'Is your pork all right Neil?' she asked. Not waiting for an answer, she addressed us:

'He has to be ever so careful about wot he eats – don't yow Neil. And he can't work – can yow Neil.'

'No.'

'No. He's got ever such a bad back. Tell them wot you've got Neil.'

'Got so many things can't remember them all.'

'He's got rheumatoid *arthurritis,* spondylitis and what's that other thing *yow've* got Neil?'

'Can't remember.'

'He had a specialist from Harley Street come to see him and he found something he didn't even know he'd got.'

'What was it Neil, he said you'd got you didn't even know you'd got?'

'Can't remember.'

'Well, whatever it was he said he'd got, he didn't even know he'd got it – did you Neil.'

'No.'

'And he's got bad knees. You've had operations on both your knees haven't you Neil.'

'Yes.'

'Course, he lives with his father-in-law.'

'We don't get on though do we Neil.'

'We're both Capricorns you see and we argue all the time.'

'Don't we Neil.'

'Yes.'

By this time I'm slightly confused. If Neil lives with his father-in-law that must be Michelle's father. And whose birth sign does she share and who does she argue with.

'I hope you don't mind me asking Michelle, but if Neil lives with his father-in-law – that must be your father?'

'Oh no, it's *his* father.'

'Ah, so it's *your* father-in-law – not his.'

'Oh yes, I suppose it is really.'

'We don't get on though do we Neil.'

'We're both Capricorns you see and we argue all the time. But he's ever so good really. Whenever we go away he looks after the dog lovely – don't he Neil.'

'Yes.'

The evening meal over, it was time for some In-house entertainment.The music struck up and people started to dance.

'I wish Neil could dance. I *luv* dancing don't I Neil.'

'I take it you don't dance then Neil?'

'No – he can't. It's his *eeps*.'

'He's had both his *eeps* done – haven't you Neil.'

'No – it wasn't me *eeps* – it was me knees.'

'Oh yes – it was his knees, but he's got to have his *eeps* done – haven't you Neil.'

The Compère announced the next dance would be a St. Bernard's Waltz.

'I can do this – I can do this,' said Michelle excitedly. 'Can yow do this Clare?'

Clare obligingly got up and did a very passable and stately St. Bernard's Waltz with Michelle, after which they started to play some rock 'n roll and the Twist, and I flung myself about recklessly, with little regard for the dignity of my years or my ancient bones. Clare must have told them how old I was for when I got back Michelle said:

'Neil, will you go up to our room and get the video camera?'

'What for?'

'I want to video this lady dancing and when I show it on me television screen I want to say to my friends: 'You see this lady dancing here – well she's 96!'

'Eighty-five, actually,' I smilingly corrected.

'Oh, sorry. Eighty-five. Yes – well. I want to say to my friends: 'See this lady dancing here –she's 96!'

'Eighty-five actually.'

'Oh yes – sorry – eighty-five.'

'*Yow'd* never know *eet* – would *yow* Neil.'

The filming never got done, for by the time poor Neil had limped up to the bedroom for the camera and limped back again, I'd danced myself off my legs and was feeling every bit the 96 years I was accused of being. So I excused myself and staggered the 100 paces and 35 stairs (which Clare, with her penchant for collecting useless information had counted) up to the bedroom, where I collapsed in a heap, and despite my 96 stroke 85 years, slept like a babe all night.

WHERE DO I FIT

Many years ago, when I was in my mid-twenties, amongst my friends was a chap called Greg. I wasn't particularly interested in him, although we went on a few dates. On one of these occasions, I remembered him saying: 'If I had to choose, I'd much prefer to be with a lady who is intelligent rather than good-looking.'

I knew I wasn't highly intelligent, but neither did I consider myself especially good-looking, so I just said, 'Oh,' and left it at that. Shortly after, he went to Germany to work with what was then known as the Allied Control Commission and we lost touch, although I heard he'd married a German girl.

Several years later, out of the blue, he telephoned me to say he was now divorced and had two grown up sons and if I was still free, would I like to go out for a meal. Intrigued, I agreed to his suggestion and over the meal we chatted about old times.

'You know Greg,' I said, raising my eyebrows, 'I remember you once saying that you would prefer to go out with someone who was intelligent rather than good-looking, but you never said which category I fitted into.'

'Oh, didn't I?' he said, and left me still wondering…

Now that I am in my nineties – it doesn't really matter anymore.

PORTRAIT OF A FANTASIST

Teresa was about seven years of age when I first got to know her. She was an engaging child, well mannered, beautifully spoken, and ever eager to impress her elders with her precocious charm. She wasn't what one might describe as a conventionally pretty child, having straight, mousy coloured hair, blue eyes that were a little too close together and rather podgy features, but her sunny nature more than made up for any lack of girly prettiness.

I got to know the family as Teresa's mother - Catlin, who was about my age, was a regular customer of the firm for which I worked and we became quite friendly, although not quite friends. When my sister visited with her two children, Chris and Susan, being of an age, Chris and Teresa would sometimes play together and because he referred to me as *Aunt*, this was the polite appellation used by Teresa when addressing me throughout the many years that I knew her.

Her parents came over to this country from Southern Ireland to find work and when I first knew them *Daddy* worked on the buses and *Mummy* worked variously as a cleaner, a doctor's receptionist, on the check-out at Tescos, or anywhere else where she could earn an honest crust.

But while Teresa's parents spoke with an unmistakable, though not unattractive Irish brogue, Teresa's manner of speech was that of a nicely educated English child.

The years went by and eventually Teresa left school and went to a Catholic teacher training college, where, to her dismay, she failed her final exams. In the meantime, her father died and she and her mother moved away to Staffordshire to live in a cottage in the grounds of a convent of which Catlin's sister was the Mother Superior.

Whether Teresa took the exams again and passed was never mentioned, but the next time she came to visit me, which was after a break of a couple of years, she told me she was teaching at a privately run Catholic school in Yorkshire, and entertained me with amusing anecdotes about some of the pupils, expertly mimicking the broad Yorkshire accent in which the children spoke. It seems that Teresa had the responsibility of advising, or encouraging the pupils in what subjects they should take as G.C.Es and one of her stories is worth repeating.

Apparently one child had no ambition or interest whatsoever in furthering her education and showed no enthusiasm for any course suggested. Finally, determined that the child would succeed at *something*, she suggested she might like to do R. E.

'Nah,' said the child. 'Ah doan't like that.'

'Why not?' asked Teresa

'I doan't like the Nun who takes it. She's daft in't she.'

'And why d'you say that?'

'Well, she tells us to close our eyes and imagine we're in a boat, then we 'ave to get out-a boat and imagine we're walking on t'water.'

'And were you able to imagine you were walking on the water?'

'Nah, I didn't get out-a bloody boat – did I.'

* * * * *

Teresa then went on to tell me that she was friendly with Peter, one of the Catholic priests attached to the school. 'He's absolutely delightful,' she enthused. 'You'd love him Aunt. Can I bring him to meet you sometime?'

'Yes, of course you can,' I replied.

Her parting shot before we said our farewells was: 'Oh, by the way – Daddy was a foreign diplomat!'

Strange – I thought after she left. I knew *daddy* had died a couple of years ago, but it was a puzzle as to how he got from working on the Midland Red buses to becoming a foreign diplomat - unless that was the job he was given when he reached his final destination. I believe God favours the Roman Catholics, but this was stretching credulity a bit too far.

I never did get to meet the lovely Peter, so at least I was spared any complicity in the deception.

The next time I saw Teresa was when she and her mother came to visit me some months later. By this time she had moved on from the school in Yorkshire and was now teaching at a girls Catholic boarding school in Sussex, where she had evidently elevated 'mummy' to the title of 'Lady' which must have been a bit risky since mummy still spoke with an easily recognisable Southern Irish brogue, with the looks, good humour and general appearance to accompany it.

They laughed as they told me Teresa had asked her mother to attend one of the schools' Open Days and, as people do on these occasions, groups of parents were standing around chatting. Then Teresa, seeing *mummy* on the fringe of a group, went over and said, 'I'm terribly sorry, I haven't introduced you – this is my mother – Lady Catlin Macintyre.'

I asked Catlin how she felt about suddenly being elevated into the upper-crust of English society, to which she impishly replied, 'Well, I wouldn't have minded if I'd known who I was supposed to be before I got there, so I could have practised my role and perhaps been more convincing. But I did my best to play the part, for to be sure, I didn't want to let me lovely daughter down. I must have carried it off quite well too, for I spent the next half hour declining the many invitations I received for lunch.'

At this point I opened a bottle of Croft Original and said we ought to drink to her newly elevated status, so we raised our glasses, clinked, and said, 'To The Lady Catlin Macintyre!'

There was more. It appears that Phillip, another school priest (it seems Teresa had a penchant for them) at some point overheard Teresa and her mother discussing whether to tax Catlin's old Ford Escort for 12 months or 6 months, it finally being decided that as it was a bit of an old banger and might not last a year, they would do it for the half year only.

Without any sense of shame, she related that when Fr. Phillip boned her and said, with some concern, 'Your father didn't leave your mother very well provided for, did he. She must be living in very reduced circumstances,' she replied, quick as a flash, 'It's not daddy's fault. I've told Mummy she really must get her priorities right. You know I told you I support a child in Africa. Well, mummy supports a whole village.'

The falsity of the statement didn't seem to trouble the conscience of either of them in the least and I grudgingly shared their admiration of Teresa's fast thinking distortion of the truth - the truth being – that *mummy* was, in reality, the impecunious widow of a God fearing, plebeian bus conductor.

.

* * * * * *

The months went by, then one day I had a telephone call from Teresa. Could she come and spend the night with me as she had an interview for the post of head mistress of a girls private Catholic school in Worcestershire and the journey there and back would be too much in one day. Naturally I agreed and when she arrived I shared her excitement and asked her to tell me all about the job and what qualified her to apply for it.

'Would you like to see my C.V?' she asked brightly.

'Love to,' I replied, as she handed me the copious folder.

'Gosh Teresa,' I said. 'I am impressed. I see you have a degree in Classics, English and French, but I don't remember a time when you were at university. And what are you teaching at your present school?'

'Classics and the Humanities, she replied, adding, 'I got my degrees through the O.U.'

I believed her. It wasn't until after she left for her interview the following morning that I began to question things in my mind. Surely someone who went to an unattached teacher training college for two years and failed her finals, was hardly bright enough to have suddenly acquired these degrees with the O.U. But then... it *must* be true. Even Teresa surely wouldn't have the nerve to make these extravagant claims when it would be easy to check their verity.

She got the job and all was well - how *could* I have doubted her. I often drove passed the school at which she was now the proud headmistress on my way back to the Midlands from Wales and we sometimes met up on a Sunday evening to go out for a meal.

She would regale me with tales of holidays spent sailing when she visited her seaside apartment in Les Issambres, South of France, and even offered my great niece Katie and her boyfriend the chance of a free holiday in her chalet if they could get the money together for the travelling. Katie eventually took her up on her offer but when it came to the crunch Teresa backed off, explaining that other people had arranged to stay on the dates given. There were many other extravagant claims she laid tongue to and I wondered sometimes if she'd quite forgotten who I was and that I'd known her and her family background for a good many years. But I mostly over-looked her fantasising, for despite all this, she could be an amusing and entertaining companion with an engaging surface charm that could fool a lot of people.

However, there was an occasion when she went a bit too far for me to take, as it involved me personally. It happened thus: Many of the children at the school owned ponies and she asked me, if she arranged for a gymkhana for them, would I be a judge for some of the classes. I agreed, but said it would only be on the condition that I would be who I was, and not a figment of her creative mind. 'Oh no. I wouldn't do that to *you* Aunt,' she charmingly assured me.

I turned up on the day with a with a friend who was stud groom at the Warwickshire Hunt, to give me some help, and was mortified to discover that I'd been described on the cover of the programme as The Hon. Miss Lynn Trowbridge. I was so angry I could barely concentrate on what I was supposed to be there for, but did my best to hide my fury, at the same time endeavouring to keep aloof from any parents who might home in on me. And I was disappointed that what could have been a very pleasant experience, in the event turned out for me, to be an embarrassing fiasco.

When it was all over and we were on our own, I told Teresa, in no uncertain terms, exactly what I thought of her and never to pull a stunt like this on me again. Then I drove off in high dudgeon, resolved that this was a friendship I didn't really need.

* * * * * *

Time passed; I moved from my home in the Midlands to Wales, decided I'd forgiven Teresa and phoned the school to give her my new address.

A no nonsense voice answered the phone and in response to my request, said sternly, 'Miss Macintyre is no longer here.'

Given the severe tone of the speaker, it didn't seem appropriate to question the reason, so I just said, 'Oh, I'm terribly sorry to have bothered you,' and put the phone down.

Intrigued, I telephoned the home of her mother. 'Yes,' said Catlin. 'She left there because she was fed-up with the responsibility of being a Head.' In response to my question as to what she was now doing, she told me that Teresa was presently working for Social Security in Birmingham, but that was only a temporary job until next term, when she would be taking a post as House Mistress at a boys prep. school in Buckinghamshire. I noticed, during our conversation, that her voice sounded a bit different and asked if she had a cold. She told me she was having treatment for cancer of the oesophagus, so I murmured my genuine sympathy and gave her my new address and telephone number for Teresa to get in touch.

I never heard from either of them again but had my own thoughts as to what might have happened.

However, there was a sort of coincidental sequence to the story. I sang with a choral society and a new member joined us who had recently moved to the area. Because she was new, I made a point of speaking with her during a break and she told me she and her friend had moved to Wales after retiring from teaching at a school (she mentioned the name of the school) in Sussex.

'Oh,' I said. 'I had a friend who once taught there – Teresa Macintyre – did you know her?'

'Yes, we did,' she said. 'Strange lady. She was very popular with the nuns and the children but thought she was too grand for the ordinary staff. Always claimed her mother was a titled 'Lady' and was always telling anyone who cared to listen about the wonderful social life she enjoyed in London at week-ends. Gill went on say that on one occasion, when she was spotted by a member of staff in a local shop, having previously let it be known that she would be attending a society function in London that week-end, she said she wasn't able to go after all, complaining that it was too bad of mummy to have forgotten to send her monthly allowance.

I have to admit I quite enjoyed listening to Gill tell more of Teresa's outrageous fantasies and took a certain amount of gossipy pleasure in revealing the truth. She must be in her early sixties now and despite all, it would give me the greatest pleasure to meet up with her again. For despite being an inveterate mythomaniac, she had an otherwise delightful personality and had inherited her mother's whimsical sense of humour. Another saving grace was that they both had the ability to laugh at themselves

Note: *The details of this account are true, but I have changed the names of the people for obvious reasons, and deliberately not identified the teacher training college and schools Teresa taught at.*

WHEN ONE ORIFICE LOOKS LIKE ANOTHER

Many years ago, long before the advent of computers and 'spell-check' I had a friend called Julie. She had completed a course in shorthand and typing and landed her first job as a secretary at a girl's boarding school.

The school was experiencing some financial difficulties and she was asked to take   shorthand notes at a meeting that had been called to discuss the best means of overcoming the present lack of funds, which were needed to carry out some essential work.

It was finally agreed that the parents would be contacted and asked, if they felt they were able to do so, to pay the school fees annually in advance instead of termly.

The letter was duly dictated, typed and despatched to the parents, but no one had noticed the typographical error requesting them to pay the fees *anally,* until the father of one pupil wrote back saying: 'No, I'd prefer to continue paying *through the nose* as I've always done.'

POST OPERATION REFLECTIONS

At first I glanced quite hopefully
But can the person glancing back
Really be me?

Take a longer look the mirror said,
For as by your reflection you are seen –
So you will be.
So I stared…
The ruthless reflection stared back,
Hostile, revealing brutal truth
Of this strangers' face
Long past its youth.
Spare me, I pleaded
With softly uttered cries,
I know back-lit mirrors
Can often tell lies,
But surely this dried out,
Sap-drained old shrew
Cannot be the person
I thought I once knew.
So much exposed of imperfection
As I regard un-misted reflection.
Lines on cheek and furrowed brow
Wrought by Natures' sneaky plough.
Blotchy, thin, age-freckled skin,
Unwanted hair on lip and chin,
Tiny blemishes here and there
Frizzy, grotty, grey-peppered hair…

The more I see of these unpalatable facts –
I wish I'd still got my cataracts.

IT'S HAPPENED AGAIN

It's happened again. Here I am in London – lost as usual. I only parked the car to get out and look for a public toilet and now I can't find it, although I'm sure it was in a side street off the main drag. And there's no public toilet where I thought there was one either. What am I doing in London anyway?

Ah, I recognise this road, don't know it's name but I *do* recognise it and I know that if I swoop off to the left at the end I'll eventually join up with the ring road which will take me to my home.

But where did I park the damned car? I flit from one unlikely place to another to search, but it's no good – I'm never going to find it and will just have to take a bus. I see no bus stop, although I'm sure there *was* one last time I was in this road.

Bewildered, I ask a passing stranger if he can tell me where the bus stop is for Leamington Spa. He looks at me as if I'm from another planet and replies, 'Never heard of the place and there ain't no bus stops in this road anyway.'

I give him a withering look and call him 'stupid' under my breath.

Then I realise I've no money to pay the fare even if there was a bus, my handbag being safely tucked under the front seat of my lost car.

I start walking. It gets dark, it is raining and the cars swoop past drowning me in spray from the gutter rivulets.

I am now on the outskirts of Coventry, some ninety odd miles from London and can't think how I got here.

Exhausted, I sink down in a shop doorway that has magically appeared before me. I pull my coat over my head for warmth, roll over and cross my legs in an effort to suppress the desperate urge to pee…but it's no good – I'll have to go.

But I am not in a shop doorway…I'm in bed.

That same damn dream (with variations) has come again, and I'm irritated that in the never-never-land of sleep, my hopeless sense of direction has once more been reinforced and magnified out of all proportion. But I am also relieved (pardon the pun) for I see my handbag is sitting innocently on the bedroom chair and a quick peep out of the window on my way back from the toilet, confirms my car is exactly where it should be – right outside my front door.

Muriel aged 18

Many readers will be familiar with my recently published memoirs 'A Life is What You Get' in which my sister – Muriel – is often mentioned.

After her death in 1998 her husband gave me two exercise books in which she had written an account of her life after leaving St. Anne's Children's Home and eventually following in my footsteps and joining the Women's Air Force.

I came across her hand-written chronicles recently when clearing out old papers and after re-reading and editing have decided they could well be of sufficient interest to be included in this book.

MURIEL'S STORY

CHAPTER 1

Education at St. Anne's Home for Waifs & Strays was rudimentary and deemed of little importance. We did not need to be educated for the future planned for us, for on leaving school at fourteen the children were sent out to work as domestic servants. However, by the time I was ready to be cast out into the big wide world things had began to change for the better. The year was 1943 and there wasn't the same demand for domestic servants as there had once been, and we were no longer forced to follow this occupation. Also, those in authority seemed to have become more enlightened and as a result, I was found a job as a telephonist at the local G.P.O.

I earned the equivalent of £2.50 per week, out of which I paid £1 a week for a drab, sparsely furnished bed-sit with a gas ring in the corner for cooking and a shared bathroom and toilet. Food was still on ration and if I bought all I was entitled to it came to 3/6 (17½p) a week. A loaf of bread was 2p and if I was careful I could make it last a week. Bread didn't seem to go mouldy in those days, it just got stale.

Not far from the Post Office there was a 'British Restaurant' where one could obtain a lunch, including a pudding, for 1/- (5p). The food was wholesome and palatable and certainly an improvement on the food at St. Anne's so I managed to get at least two decent cooked meals a week.

Although now free from the strict regime of the Home, life didn't suddenly become easy and carefree. I was often lonely and always hard-up and lived in fear of my grim-faced landlady. Unlike now, one could be thrown out of one's lodgings on the slightest whim. I was once threatened with eviction for hanging a pair of black silk knickers on the bathroom rail to dry.

I loved those knickers. My sister Lynn had sent them to me as part of a birthday present when she was stationed in Cairo. As clothes were still on ration they were a treasured possession, but I was not prepared for the furore this simple act caused. The other people living in the house besides the landlady were her husband and an elderly male lodger, and I was accused of trying to incite them into debauchery, although I think her words were a bit more basic than the ones I've used. Nothing could have been further from the truth, but I never wore those knickers again until I got married some years later.

It was difficult having friends, as visitors were not encouraged; but the room was so shabbily furnished and dreary that I would have been reluctant to invite anyone back anyway. So I tended to keep myself to myself and was often accused by my colleagues of being aloof.

Things improved when Lynn came back from abroad and I was able to spend some Sundays with her, when we would share a meagre meal and a Sunday newspaper, not necessarily for the news content but so that we could read the book reviews, decide which one we would like to read, then one of us would go the library and suggest they add it to their shelves. Lynn had also bought a wireless, so we would often listen to music, radio plays etcetera. Other than this though, we didn't really have a lot in common and I didn't want to intrude too much on her way of life.

So it was a happy day when Eileen, one of the girls with whom I worked, persuaded me to go to a Saturday night hop with her at the local dance hall. This became a regular Saturday entertainment, spoiled by the fact that I always had to leave early as my landlady locked and bolted the front door at 10.30pm and if I wasn't back before then I wouldn't be able to get in.

After a while I finally confessed to Eileen why I always had to leave early and told her a bit about the circumstances I was living under. She had already begun asking me round to her parents' house on a Sunday for a meal and I would take what I could of my rations to help out with the food. It was such a lovely experience being accepted into the bosom of a family and made a welcome change from staying in my dreary bed-sit all day in the winter months, hoping I wouldn't run out of pennies to feed the voracious appetite of the gas meter.

After enjoying the friendship of Eileen and her family, it came as a shock when she told me that her father, who worked on the railways, had been promoted to Station Master and they would be moving up North. When I visited the following Sunday they talked about their proposed move, but I found it hard to share their enthusiasm about the move, and felt close to tears when I thought how much I would miss them.

My sadness was soon dispelled however when they asked me if I'd like to go with them. They said they'd been to see the station master's house; it was large and they were sure there would be room for me if I thought I might like to join them. Eileen was all for it and said it would be lovely to have a ready made friend in their new place.

She had already managed to secure a transfer with the GPO and I said I would love to go with them if I could get a transfer too. So I applied, but was disappointed in their response, to be told that there were no vacancies at the present time, but that I would be invited to re-apply should a vacancy occur in the future when my application would be given favourable consideration.

I was crestfallen, but when I told Eileen's parents I didn't really want to move without having a job to go to they said I was not to worry as they were sure I would soon find one and I could stay with them as long as it suited. Lynn didn't agree, and said I would be silly to give up my job and that I should wait until I got confirmation or otherwise of a transfer as a telephonist before making up my mind. The matter was finally settled after Lynn was invited to meet the family and after talking with them she said she felt more comfortable about me joining them.

So, after weighing up the pros and cons, and with Lynn's grudging agreement, I finally decided to make the move. When the time came to go, I had mixed feelings and wondered if I was doing the right thing and worried about what the future might hold. But it was too late now for second thoughts - I'd burned my boats and I must condition myself to face whatever the future might hold.

It was a bit of a shock to me when we arrived in Oldham. It was a dark, Lancashire town, which I learned later had been thrown up during the Industrial Revolution. The older parts had cobbled streets, small, back to back houses and factories everywhere, which were belching out copious clouds of smoke which seemed to cast a film of black soot over everything. It reminded me of Blake's *dark satanic mills*, although the cotton mills were, in some cases, quite architecturally majestic and built on moors which surrounded the town.

Eileen's parents' house, by comparison with many of the houses in Oldham, was fairly large and situated on the edge of the town. It had a garden back and front and three bedrooms and I was very happy to have been allotted a nice, cosy little bedroom to call my own, even if it was, understandably, the smallest and furthest from the bathroom. After helping to unpack and arrange furniture etcetera, I already began to feel part of the family and thought once I'd got a job I could settle quite happily.

The day after arriving and for several ensuing days I applied for jobs, but I was either deemed too young, too inexperienced, or the vacancy had already been filled. Hope stirred one day when I actually got as far as being taken round a cotton mill, where the noise of the machines was so deafening, the workers seemed only able to communicate by signing or lip reading. When I emerged from the factory I was covered in fluff from head to toe, and was not too disappointed when I wasn't offered the job.

Then, walking back one dark evening, feeling low and dispirited after another fruitless day of job hunting, I was suddenly startled by what I thought was a stampede of horses bearing down on me. I threw my arms up to protect my head and ran for the shelter of a shop doorway. It was a relief when I realised the 'stampede' was nothing more than the clatter of wooden clogs on cobbles, worn by the workers pouring out of a local factory.

After several days of fruitless searching for a job I got so worried and dispirited, I decided to apply to join the WAAF. Although the war was over there were still posters everywhere advertising for girls to join up and in desperation I sent off for an enlistment form, which I filled in and posted. In the meantime, I continued to apply for jobs and eventually I was taken on at a factory, working on the assembly line fastening bicycle toe clips together with nuts and bolts.

The work was tedious and boring; my nails got broken, my fingers were sore and ingrained with grease and dirt and my feet ached from standing all day. But I wasn't complaining – it was a job, and I could now pay more to Eileen's mother for my board and lodging although, not by a word or a look had she ever indicated that I wasn't still welcome in their home.

The women I worked with were friendly enough, though rough and ready and often sang or recited risqué verses or told rude jokes which mostly went over my head, but I always laughed so they wouldn't think me either stupid or superior. There were times though, when I was caught out in my naivety. On one occasion a woman was reciting (presumably for my benefit) a rude ditty, one line of which sounded like: *She gave him sickness and diarrhoea.*

'Ha-ha,' I laughed in mock amusement, 'Fancy writing a poem about someone making somebody ill.'

There were puzzled looks until I repeated what I thought I'd heard, then hoots of raucous laughter ensued when it was explained that the line was from a poem (?) called 'Eskimo Nell' and what he'd been given was *syphilis and gonorrhoea.* At that time I didn't even know what this was, but not wishing to show my ignorance I laughed along with the rest of them and resolved to look the words up as soon as I had time to visit a library.

I remember an occasion when a screwdriver I was using slipped and dug into my hand. 'Damn and blast!' I yelled, as I shook my hand in pain and anger.

'Eeh, don't she swear posh,' said a woman standing near me.

After I'd learned to understand the broad Lancashire dialect and accustomed myself to the bawdy banter of my workmates, I got to quite like them, for despite their coarse humour, there was a genuine friendliness and a desire to be helpful. And it is possible that my falsely cultivated '*GPO Telephonist*' voice was just as foreign to their ears as I found their manner of speaking to mine.

It was not long before my friend Eileen found herself a young man and although I was pleased for her, I also felt twinges of envy, mainly because it deprived me of her company some evenings, but also because I wished I had a nice boy friend, although where I was to find one I had no idea – certainly not in my work place.

Then one day a letter came from the GPO to say there was a vacancy for a telephonist in Manchester and in view of my previous experience I was invited to apply. I was tempted, but as I had already sent off the forms to join the air force I thought

I might as well stay where I was and struggle on with my nuts and bolts.

A few anxious weeks passed before the eagerly awaited letter from the RAF Recruiting Centre in Manchester arrived inviting me to attend for an interview and medical.

CHAPTER 2

I asked for the day off work and duly presented myself at the Recruiting Centre where there were about eight other girls waiting. A stern looking N.C.O. told us to remove all our clothing and sit on a bench in this long, narrow corridor, with just our coats on.

We all felt vulnerable and exposed sitting there, practically nude, in a strange, bleak place with total strangers and some of the girls chickened out right there and then. But I'd come this far, considered my options, and decided to stick with it.

We had to give our medical history and all I could remember, apart from the usual ailments, was the pneumonia and lung abscess I'd had when I was about four or five years old. They also asked the medical history of my parents and I had to confess I couldn't tell them much as they'd both died of tuberculosis when I was a child.

We were given an X-ray and then went to see the job selection officer. The results of various intelligence tests would determine what trades we were suitable for. I had put my civilian job down as a telephonist, but the selection officer said I had done so well in the intelligence tests, he thought I was capable of doing something much better than that. 'How would I like to train as a Radio Telephony Operator?'

I asked what that entailed and he said it was like the Air Force equivalent of a civilian Air Traffic Controller. It would involve talking to pilots by radio and giving them take-off and landing instructions; logging conversations and working on direction findings etcetera. In fact, it was the job of the girl on the recruiting poster.

Oh yes – I'd seen that poster. There was this attractive WAAF with a superior look standing next to an RAF man dressed in air crew gear. It said something like 'Serve in the WAAF with the men who fly. The RAF needs girls like you.' I'd seen that sort of thing in war films too. Yes, I'd definitely like to be an RT/OP. They said I would hear in a week or two provided my medical was satisfactory.

I floated back to Oldham on air and reported to Eileen and her parents the events of the day. They were pleased for me but I decided to say nothing at work until I had confirmation of my acceptance, although I did write to Lynn and give her my news. She wrote back to say how pleased she was and that it would be the making of me.

A letter arrived some days later, but instead, as anticipated, confirming that I had been accepted, it requested me to go for further medical tests, as apparently a shadow had appeared on the X-ray of my lungs. I was disappointed and scared, but kept the drawback to myself and reported back to Manchester as requested.

After a second X-ray it was decided that as I had no other symptoms of illness, what appeared to be a 'shadow' on my lung was most likely scarring from the childhood abscess. I could have cried with relief.

Then one week, two weeks, three weeks dragged by. Didn't they want me to be one of the girls on the poster after all. And what a fool I'd been not to go for the Post Office telephonist job. To add to my woes, I caught the most awful cold and began to imagine that I might, indeed, have a serious illness after all.

Towards the end of the fourth week, I couldn't stand the suspense any longer and rang the recruiting office to enquire about the delay. They assured me I would be hearing soon and after a few further anxious weeks I was asked to report to RAF Wilmslow on 15th August 1947 for basic training. This was exactly six years to the day after Lynn had joined.

My factory workmates insisted on taking me out for a farewell drink. It was a Saturday night and the pub we went to had a man playing an accordion, who invited anyone who had a mind to join him on the raised dais to sing a song or tell a few jokes. I was asked to 'do a turn' but not having a pushy nature refused, protesting that the only sort of songs I knew would not go down well in a noisy pub.

'What do you know?' asked the accordionist.

'Bach/Gounod's Ave Maria' I said diffidently, fairly sure that he wouldn't know it. (I'd learned it by listening to Deana Durban singing it on a gramophone record at St.Anne's and used to sing it as my party piece to the visiting committee ladies,.

The man on the accordion nodded and began to play the introductory bars and before I knew it, I found myself up on the dais. Made brave by the effects of the unaccustomed amount of port and lemon I'd imbibed, I took temporary leave of my inhibitions and began to sing. I was aware that the pub had become quiet, which was unnerving, but there was no stopping now, so I gave it all I got and hoped I'd manage to reach the top note without faltering. I did, was voted the best 'turn' of the night and was rewarded with £2 and a free drink on the house.

As I walked home with Eileen and her boyfriend when the evening was over I felt happier than I'd felt for a very long time. (I never sang Ave Maria again, except in the bath, but whenever I hear it sung it always brings back fond memories of that night of brief glory).

The next day I bade Eileen and her lovely parents farewell, and with fervent promises to keep in touch, climbed aboard the train to take me to RAF Wilmslow.

And so ended another chapter of my brief life as I sped along in the train to greet the next.

CHAPTER 3

I arrived at RAF Wilmslow with a toothbrush, a comb, a few other toiletries, some make-up and the clothes I stood up in and hoped it wouldn't be too long before they issued us with a uniform.

There were about thirty of us reported for training and we were shown our quarters in purpose built huts, each containing sixteen single beds and a round, tall, black-leaded stove which stood in the middle. Then we were taken to the Mess, where we enjoyed a good lunch, after which we were taken to the Equipment Centre to be measured for our uniforms.

We were told we would be given three days to make up our minds whether we really wanted to be in the WAAF after which it would be too late. My mind was already made up and I was prepared to make the best of things whatever happened. After three days, those of us who wished to stay were required to sign on for the "Duration of the Present Emergency." As the war was over, I couldn't quite fathom what the present emergency was, or how long it was likely to last, but I was glad there was one and that it needed me.

To my surprise, we were told we would have to undergo another medical before commencing training and the following afternoon were informed that everyone had passed except for an Irish girl and me. I was shocked and frightened as I reported for yet another X-ray and further tests. The nurse told us soothingly not to worry as we might have moved and spoiled the X-ray and to keep perfectly still this time. But this did nothing to still my thumping heart.

I was asked if I had a cough, did I sweat at night, did I tire easily or feel generally unwell. Although I was truthfully able to answer 'no' to all these questions, I couldn't help but worry that they had detected something wrong with me and I sat there, scared and miserable, wondering what on earth I would do if they finally rejected me on health grounds. I prayed that I hadn't got T.B. but even if I hadn't, suppose they found me medically unfit for service for some other reason. I had no home, no job and no plans now other than to be in the WAAF.

After an anxious wait that seemed like an eternity, the nurse came back and said I was all right. What they had seen was the healed scar on my left lung that had previously been detected. Then she added that to be on the safe side they would .. (oh no – not reject me!) grade me medically B2 and that I must report sick immediately if I had any chest trouble. I didn't care how they graded me as long as they let me stay. The poor Irish girl was found to have heart trouble and was sent back to her home in Belfast.

So I was now to become 2801511 Aircraft Woman Trowbridge and to swear faithfully to serve His Majesty King George V1 and his heirs and successors. For record purposes, we were required to give our home address, but this presented another problem as I hadn't really got one. I considered putting 'No Fixed Abode' but then recalled how much we resented being described as 'Waifs & Strays' at St. Anne's and I had no wish to authenticate this description. Although I was demonstrably no longer a Waif, to have recorded on my documents: "No Fixed Abode" might well imply I was still a Stray so I gave Lynn's address and entered her as my next of kin.

We were issued with our kit and told to mark and zealously guard it, as any deficiencies would have to replaced at our own expense. We were given an inventory and every item was quaintly suffixed with the words: 'Airwoman for the use of.' The issue brassieres', instead of being cut with an uplift, were cut in a downward curve designed to flatten our natural contours. The corsets had stiff bones in front which dug into my ribs when sitting or bending, so I removed them and hoped my act of vandalism would not be discovered. Aside from keeping our figures in order, the corsets were also to keep our stockings up and we were told on no account were we to wear garters for this purpose as they could cause varicose veins. Whoever decreed this must have over-looked the fact that our sturdy knickers had elasticated legs. Even so, to make sure the rule wasn't flouted, there would be random inspections, when we would be ordered to lift our skirts to make sure we weren't wearing garters. We had two uniforms, one of which was to be kept for best and only worn on ceremonial occasions and the other for every day wear. Our shirts had detachable collars which we took to the Chinese Laundry to be washed and starched. They would come back shiny and stiff as a board and often dug into our necks making them rough and sore, but we would prefer to suffer this than be seen with a soft, curling collar. (I learned later, to my horror, that the workers at Chinese laundries allegedly spat on the collars to stiffen them, but then comforted myself with the thought that this couldn't be true, unless all the staff at the laundry suffered with chronic bronchitis in order to provide enough phlegm for this practice). A black tie, peaked cap and heavy, black lace-up shoes completed the ensemble.

Someone in authority had decided that all skirt hems should measure sixteen inches from the ground so they all looked the same length when we were marching. This was all very well for the taller girls whose skirts could be inches below their knees, but for someone like me at five foot nothing, the skirt seemed almost indecently short and I was frequently advanced upon by keen NCO's with measuring sticks, who were disappointed to find I was regulation length.

Despite these seemingly petty rules and regulations, I felt proud and happy to be wearing the uniform and actually enjoyed the drill and marching that was all part of the training.

At lectures we were given the history and structure of the RAF and told the motto - Per Ardua Astra meant: *Through Endeavour to the Stars.* How romantic and inspiring I thought, then came down to earth with a bump when we were told that it took two airwomen to equal one airman on the staffing strength of a station. So it was official – women were inferior to men – although I believe this equation no longer exists in the services.

We had a real bully of a sergeant, whose male counterpart I've often seen portrayed in films. She would bawl obscenities at us for no apparent reason and even suggested that if we thought someone wasn't pulling their weight, they should be tossed into a bath of cold water to teach them a lesson. This actually happened to one poor hapless wretch in another billet, her crime being that she'd walked across the floor of the hut with her outside shoes on after it had been polished.

We each had responsibility for our own bed space and immediate surroundings, which had to be polished and dusted every day, with collective responsibility for the general areas. This presented no hardship to me, although there were sometimes arguments about this, but they were usually amicably resolved as we knew it was in our best interests to work as a team. Our mattresses were made up of three squares known as 'biscuits' and when not being slept on, they had to be stacked neatly on top of each other, with sheets and blankets being folded to exactly the same size and placed over the *biscuits* with the flattened pillow on top. Everything had to be in exact alignment – mattresses, bedding, spare shoes, brushes, tooth brushes etcetera – all in one straight line right down the hut. We would spend ages telling each other to move things slightly forward or back and we would check each others efforts to make sure everything was in perfect order for inspection. Then we would stand 'at ease' by our beds, tremulously awaiting the arrival of the bullying sergeant.

At her approach, we would be brought smartly to attention and brace ourselves for whatever was to come. She would stride into the hut, eyes darting all over the place. A long, accusing finger would reach out and, as if by magic, find an offending speck of dust that had escaped our assiduous attentions. It was a point of honour with her that fault must be found and if she could find no dust, then some hapless person would be accused of 'poor alignment' and their carefully arranged equipment would be unceremoniously trashed. This always evinced sympathy from the rest of us and bonded us even closer in our collective dislike of the spiteful sergeant.

The 'square bashing' was endless and exhausting but I took to it very well. We marched everywhere, even to breakfast, and spent hours drilling on the Parade Ground. To get into formation we had to line up, tallest on the right, shortest on the left. I knew my place as there was no one shorter than me, though it would have been nice to have someone to look down on once in a while instead of always having to look up to. At first we had to shout the marching timing: Halt, one two. About turn, one pause, two pause, three pause, four. When they decided we were proficient enough to stop shouting, invariably someone would forget and call out the sequence, which made us all want to giggle, but which seemed to enrage the Drill Sergeant almost to the point of apoplexy.

Airmen's arms had only to be swung waist high, but it was decided the WAAF would look more impressive if the swing was exaggerated to shoulder height, and I think this style of marching is maintained to this day. One of the girls had difficulty coordinating her arm and leg movements and was constantly being bawled out. She finally managed to overcome this, but not her habit of leaning forward when she marched, whereas we were supposed to be proudly upright.

On one occasion the exasperated drill Sergeant yelled out, ''Buckingham, your marching is shocking and your bottom sticks out!'

'Yes Sergeant – I'll correct that,' she responded, bending even further forward.

'Then do it now!' bawled the Sergeant.

'Yes, I will,' replied Buckingham, this time eagerly jutting her jaw forward as well.

For once the Sergeant was left speechless and rolled her eyes to heaven in despair, but I'm sure I saw the hint of a smile when we were finally told to "Fall out!"

We were not allowed to leave the confines of the camp for three weeks, until they made sure we were sufficiently well trained and smart enough to wear our uniform in public. We were forbidden to eat sweets or ice cream, or smoke cigarettes in the street, but as I'd never done any of these things anyway, it was no hardship.

We were drilled in guard duty and told how, if we were on duty and someone approached the station at night we must shout, "Halt! Who goes there – friend or foe?"

If the answer was "Friend" we had to shout, "Advance and be recognised."

I can't remember what we were supposed to do if anyone was foolish enough to answer "Foe." We certainly couldn't shoot them as they didn't issue us with guns.

As an adjunct to our training we were taught to be health conscious and to refrain from any activities which might be detrimental to our physical wellbeing. We were shown a graphic, technicolor film about V.D. which shocked us to the core. Brightly coloured diagrams of healthy, internal organs were displayed, then we saw the same organs turning dark red, then yellow as inflammation and infection spread. It looked frightening and dreadful as they continued to the bitter end with general paralysis of the insane to the final calamity – death!

I was so horrified, I decided sex definitely wasn't for me, not until I was safely married anyway. It was probably meant to have this effect, as during my time in the Service only one girl got pregnant and one got V.D. from her American boy friend.

There was no mention of birth control or safe sex in those days – nice girls didn't do it and that was that. I once wrote to a popular woman's magazine to ask about birth control before I was about to get married. They sent me a snooty reply stating that advice would not be made available to single women and I must wait until I was married, when I could write again and they would give me the information I required. How times have changed, but I sometimes wonder if for the better.

Despite the rigorous discipline of our initial training, I was beginning to settle down well into my new life and felt secure and safe in this structured and purposeful environment. It was good also to have the companionship of women who came from all walks of life and were, on the whole, a pretty decent bunch, even if there were a few rough diamonds.

My particular friend was Molly McNamara from Birkenhead. She told me she had joined up to escape her social environment as she hated being referred to as Liverpool Irish. She wished to be known as 'Frankie' a name curiously at odds with her stunning, feminine appearance. She had thick, wavy auburn hair, was incredibly good looking and had a figure to die for. Men flocked around her but she disdained them and confessed she didn't know what it was to have a crush on anyone.

As new recruits we were paid thirty shillings a week (£1.50) and received it fortnightly. Having had to feed, clothe myself and pay for heating, rent, etcetera on not much over this amount in the past, I felt quite well off, considering uniform, food and accommodation were all free. And being a non-smoker, I managed very well on the money and was even able to save a little. Even though *I* considered the pay adequate, there were those who couldn't always make it last and the frequent lament of one of the trainees, a Scottish girl with a broad Glaswegian accent was: 'A've nae bloody money and nae bloody fags - can anyone gee me a wee drag of their stub?'

Our basic training over, we had our Passing Out Parade. The majority of the airwomen had relatives to come and witness the occasion and I wished I had someone, but as Frankie didn't have anyone either, I didn't mind too much.

The following day we were dispersed to our various RAF Stations for our trade or professional training.

CHAPTER 4

Frankie and I were supposed to do our radio telephony course at RAF Cranwell, but as there was going to be a delay of three months or more we were posted to Bomber Command at Leeming Bar in Yorkshire for work experience and to give us an insight into the rudiments of the job before our official training.

We were pleased to find that our accommodation was far less sparse than at Wilmslow. We had the luxury of central heating and did not have to endure frequent billet inspections. Part of our work remit was to go into the aircraft hangers to see if the aircraft radios were working properly. The first time I had to do this I was told to call the control tower. I eagerly climbed into the aircraft cockpit and examined the dials in front of me. One of the many dials said: 'Press to talk' and another 'Press to fire.'

No problem I thought, until I was warned that a WAAF had once pressed the wrong button and had the airmen racing for cover as she sprayed the hangar with ammunition. With this piece of information ringing in my ears, I was so nervous I couldn't stop my hands from trembling and was barely able to get out the words: 'Leeming Tower from R.T.O. testing, testing, how do you receive me? - Over.'

They answered, 'Loud and clear.'

I replied, 'Roger out,' and sank back in the cockpit with a huge sigh of relief.

We spent a lot of our working time logging, which meant writing down everything that was said between aircraft and control in an abbreviated code. This was tedious and boring as we couldn't actually see any of the action from the room in which we were closeted. However, we had some fun jobs too, like when we were told to smash up surplus or unserviceable equipment. We were ordered to do this rather than let it get into the wrong hands and I used to enjoy myself with my little hammer smashing up valves and transformers and things. By way of diversion we would sometimes play mock duels with redundant aerials which were shaped a bit like swords. We mimicked the traditional challenge of the airmen which was: Aerials for two – coffee for one.' I hasten to add that no one actually came to grief during these foolhardy skirmishes, although there were some near misses.

The one thing I wanted to do was fly and I was fortunate enough to be in one of those trades that would allow WAAF to do this. Even so, it had to be for a legitimate reason, such as testing the radio or intercom or something, and written permission had to be obtained from the commanding officer.

So I applied for permission, which was granted, and the following day I was fitted with a parachute and climbed aboard a Wellington Bomber. It was quite exciting taking off, but after that I got no sensation of flying at all. It was a dull day and there was nothing to see but grey cloud, black cloud and yet more cloud. There were about six or eight in the crew and I became disenchanted and bored after I'd done a perfunctory check on the communications system. The noise of the engines was so loud that conversation was almost impossible and we just sat, glumly staring at each other.

Then someone managed to convey to me that we were turning back because of engine trouble. Great, I thought, that will make things a bit more exciting, and I don't remember feeling at all scared. As we approached the airfield and began to descend, I got the most dreadful pain in my ears and thought my head was about to burst. One of the crew members sitting opposite had the most enormous Flying Officer Kite moustache. Aware of my discomfort, he was miming to me to do a chewing motion to ease the pressure in my ears. Despite my discomfort I had to laugh at how ludicrous he looked waggling his monstrous moustache up and down.

We landed safely after a few unnerving bumps over the landing strip, but I wasn't put off and thereafter flew in Wellingtons as often as I could obtain permission, even though the flights were seldom without some minor incident or other. On one occasion, disaster struck as I was about to leave the plane. The hook on the parachute caught on something and pulled the release mechanism. The parachute billowed out and seemed to fill the plane, smothering the crew behind me. Highly embarrassed, I scrabbled it as best I could into my arms and shamefacedly dragged it to the hanger to be re-packed.

One day one of the pilots said that if he took me up in his plane I would never want to fly again. I accepted the challenge and climbed into a little two-seater plane which I think was either a Martinet or Tiger Moth. We swooped around in the air, banking, stalling, ascending, and diving, the while my stomach went up to my ears and down to my boots. This was really good fun and just how I'd always imagined flying would be. When we landed the white faced pilot asked me how I felt.

'That was marvellous, I feel absolutely fine,' I replied happily.

'Well I don't. I feel bloody terrible,' he groaned and staggered off to be sick.

The story must have circulated round some of the RAF Stations, for when, some months later, I was in the NAAFI canteen in Lincoln, an aircrew sergeant, whom I didn't know, came over to me and said to his companions: 'Well can you believe it? Here she is – the girl I was telling you about. The one old Trevor tried to frighten and ended up being as sick as a dog himself.'

I felt quite pleased with my little spot of notoriety and for once, enjoyed being the centre of attention instead of my glamorous friend - Frankie. We were the only two girls working in the Radar Section, but we got on well with the men and went around in a sort of happy gang. Going to the pictures was one of the most popular off-duty pastimes. There were also dances on camp on a Saturday night with a very good RAF Band playing in the Glenn Miller style. They always played "Who's Taking You Home Tonight" as the last waltz, and I used to get teased about this. Spectacles weren't very flattering in those days and my friends told me I looked more attractive without them. So I left them off when we went dancing. The trouble was, being short-sighted, I couldn't distinguish clearly the features of the person I might be dancing with, unless I peered very closely into their faces and the near sighted gazing was often mistaken for romantic interest, which was often not the case.

In the end, I decided to forget vanity, ignore the advice of my friends, and wear my glasses all the time. I have to say it didn't seem to make an appreciable difference to the level of my popularity or otherwise and I could now disregard the writer – Dorothy Parker's cruel couplet "Men seldom make passes at girls who wear glasses."

CHAPTER 5

The RAF was very keen on sport and every Wednesday afternoon was dedicated to the pursuit of this. Unless we were doing something absolutely vital, work had to be abandoned and one was obliged to indulge in some form of physical activity.

I was not a particularly athletic or sporty person, but had played a bit of schoolgirl hockey, so this was my form of exercise, apart from the obligatory supervised physical jerks. I was surprised and pleased that I was allowed me to keep my glasses on to play, as at school I had to take them off and could hardly see the ball, never mind the person I was supposed to pass it to.

Our sports organiser was a Flight Officer Sanger-Davies – a really jolly hockey stick type. She asked me if I was related to the former Corporal Trowbridge and when I confirmed that she was, indeed my sister, she clapped me heartily on the back and said that if I was half as good at sport as her, I'd be all right. Soon the strength of my sister's athletic ability I was picked for the station hockey team, even though I didn't consider myself to be much good. But I did my best to respond to her rallying cries of 'Come on you forwards! Run, tackle!'

So I ran, up and down the pitch until my lungs were fit to burst and tackled as furiously as I knew how, being more terrified of incurring the displeasure of the worthy F/O Sanger-Davies than anything a retaliating, ankle chopping, over zealous opponent could do to me.

We played at various RAF Stations and the home team entertained the visiting team to tea afterwards with something really special – like sausage, chips and peas.

Then we played a really important match. If we won this it would qualify us to play against Scotland and if we won that match, we would play against Ireland. We *did* win and drove back to camp in RAF transport happily singing, over and over again, 'If you ever go across the sea to Ireland.' We really looked forward to that match in Scotland.

When the time came we caught the famous Flying Scotsman at York and travelled to RAF Pitreavie Castle, Scotland. The train was full and we charged up and down the corridors with our hockey sticks trying to find seats, feeling very important and getting in everyone's way. F/O Sanger-Davies had been given the equivalent of just over 22p a head to buy us a cup of tea and a bite to eat, so we were anxious to be near her and the buffet car.

We travelled on the Tuesday, were to play on the Wednesday and travel back on the Thursday, so we looked on it as an adventure and were full of hope and exuberance. We even threw a few coppers into the water for luck as we crossed the Forth Bridge.

Our reception at Pitreavie Castle was anything but welcoming. We were given accommodation in the same type of dreadful old huts we'd been in at Wilmslow, but now it was winter and very cold. The same standard black stove stood in the middle of the hut, but it had not been ignited and it was not until after our arrival that a match was put to it. But it was reluctant to burn, despite our raking and cursing and coaxing. So after an indifferent meal in the station canteen, we spent the rest of the evening shivering around the un-cooperative black stove, cheering ourselves up by swigging from a couple of bottles of cider that the worthy Sanger-Davies had thoughtfully provided. It was pretty rough stuff, but at least it made us giggly and less aware of the bleakness and discomfort of our billet.

When we got up the next morning the weather was appalling. It was January and snowing, raining and blowing a gale all at the same time. There was some speculation that the match might have to be postponed, but the conditions might worsen and we could hardly stay here indefinitely. It had cost the limited funds of the station such a lot to send us, we would just *have* to play.

No such thing as track suits in those days, so we set off to walk to the pitch in our little short sleeve sports shirts, short navy skirts and a cardigan, to be removed when play started. We were frozen, soaked through and thoroughly demoralised before we even started the hockey match, and even the hearty Sanger-Davies looked pinched and less than her usual, enthusiastic self.

The other team arrived snugly cloaked in their ground sheets – a sort of large, waterproof cape, which could also be used to spread on the ground when sleeping under canvas. They were part of standard equipment, but ordinarily, no one would be seen dead wearing one. Oh how we wished we'd had the forethought to bring ours now.

We assembled on the pitch to commence battle and saw their goalie take up her position. She was a huge, fat Warrant Officer, and her intimidating presence seemed to fill the whole of the area between the goal posts. By contrast, our goalie was a tall, slim, elegant corporal with a languid, ladylike manner. She was the reserve, for our usual goalkeeper had succumbed to a bout of diarrhoea.

We 'bullied-off' (as one did in those days) and in no time at all the area around the opposition goal was a mass of slimy mud, but no matter how we tried, we could not get the ball past that giant of a goalkeeper. I raced up and down that pitch, heart pounding, fighting for breath, tackling and hacking and whacking, all to no avail. Exhausted by our efforts to attack, we were almost too weak to defend and they had no difficulty at all in getting the ball past our languid lady corporal. We changed ends with the score 3 – 0 to them. We then churned up the mud at the other end of the field, but despite the rallying cries of our captain and her heroic efforts, we still failed to get the ball past that menacing, omnipotent goalkeeper.

They scored again and our distraught goalie overheard one of our exasperated defenders complain that she wasn't even trying, whereupon she burst into tears, and continued to weep whilst more goals whizzed past her.

The final, humiliating score was 7 – 0 and we trudged off the pitch mortified, mud-spattered and miserable and decided we definitely didn't like Scotland. Our dream of playing a match in Ireland being ignominiously shattered, I never could muster the same enthusiasm for hockey again and I think I was a bitter disappointment to the estimable Miss Sanger-Davies. When the time came for Frankie and I to leave Leeming Bar and embark on our official training course at RAF Cranwell, we were seen off at the railway station by her with much bonhomie, shouts of 'good luck!' and vigorous waving as the train puffed its way out, carrying me on to yet another chapter in my life.

CHAPTER 6

We knew it would be different at Cranwell. It was a massive station and was known as *The Cradle of the Royal Air Force.* There was a college which trained young officers to become pilots; an Apprentice School, a school for radio mechanics and radio fitters and Number One Radio School, which we were to attend.

After our fairly laid-back time at Leeming Bar, it was now down to work with a vengeance and we spent the next three months studying eight hours a day. We learned such things as Faraday's Law on electro magnetic induction; Lenz's Law on the theory of alternating magnetic fields; the electro-magnetic field corkscrew rule; the velocity of electro-magnetic waves etcetera. Strange new words such as triode, tetrode, pentrode and many more were now all part of our working vocabulary and the more I learned, the more confidence I gained.

After being brain-washed at St. Anne's for so many years to believe we would none of us amount to anything much, it was especially pleasing to have this opportunity to study and at the end of the training I was thrilled to achieve a 98% pass mark in the exams, which, I was told, had never before been accomplished by either men or women and I was given immediate promotion to Leading Aircraft Woman.

So here I was – a *somebody* at last. I'd reached the pinnacle of my present ambition and could hold my head up proudly with the girl on the Advertising Poster where I had wanted to be for so long.

I remained in the WAAF until I met and married Gordon – a Naval Petty Officer –and started a family. Two children, a divorce, re-marriage and one more child I can still look back and truthfully say my years in the WAAF were amongst the happiest of my life.

FRINGE BELIEFS

My sister, wasn't really much into church going in her adult years, except for special occasions like weddings, christenings and funerals, although she liked singing hymns and we could both get quite emotional about televised Remembrance Services and the like.

However, in middle-life she did have a spell of attending Spiritualist Meetings which were held in the Labour Hall at Minster on the Isle of Sheppey. On one of my visits she asked me to go along with her. I was sceptical about the whole thing and wondered what she hoped to get out of it. She couldn't have expected to get a message from the dead as, apart from our parents, (long since dead), we neither of us knew anyone who was likely to want to contact us from the grave.

I went along anyway, partly to please her and partly out of curiosity and was singularly unimpressed with the whole experience. It was a kind of informal service, conducted by a slightly dotty-looking middle-aged lady. We sang a few hymns, accompanied on a hopelessly out of tune piano, and these were interspersed with a few made-up prayers, then we all said the 'Our Father,' before the dotty lady metamorphosed herself into '*Medium mode.*'

With an open mind, I sat up and took notice, ready to be impressed or otherwise, and waited, with bated breath, to see ectoplasm exuding from her orifices, as she staggered about the stage in a trancelike attitude.

Nothing as dramatic as this happened, but eventually, after much staggering and forehead rubbing, she declared that someone with initial "F" had come through for an elderly lady who was sitting near me. I was so amused with what took place next, that I versified the incident afterwards and read it to Muriel.

I was disappointed when she didn't seem to share my irreverent sense of humour, her only comment being that she thought the lady's coat was green, not red..

'It was,' I replied testily, 'but *green* wouldn't have rhymed with *head*, *said*, *dead* and Fred, so it had to be *red*.'

'But it was *green* actually.' she persisted.

THE MEDIUM

The Medium fingered her puzzled head,
Then hesitantly, haltingly, hand-pointing said,
'I'm coming to you dear, the lady in red,
Are you receiving me?'
'It's you she means Mum.'
'Who luv – me? I'll just get me glasses
For I really can't see.'
'Now you'll have to speak up dear,
I'm a little bit deaf.'

'Do you know anyone with initial "F"?'
'Can you speak a bit louder, I really can't hear.'
'Someone with initial "F" wants to contact you dear.'

The old lady rummaged but did not seem
To know what initial "F" could mean.
'You *do* know,' nudged daughter, 'It's me Uncle Fred,'
'Oh *him*,' said myopic, deaf lady in red.
No, it can't be him – I thought he was dead.'

THE CHEERFUL GIVERS

Church of St. Thomas the Apostle, Harty Ferry

On one of my visits to the Isle of Sheppey in Kent my sister suggested I might like to drive to the little Church of St. Thomas the Apostle at Harty Ferry, a remote, isolated spot on the island. To reach it we had to drive along a single track road flanked on either side by the Kent marshes until we eventually reached the tiny hamlet.

It was worth the journey for the church was quite delightful, set, as it was, but a matter of yards from the coast with enchanting views all round. On entering the church, I was immediately struck by its simple beauty and captivating sense of tranquillity and despite its remoteness, it was obviously a well loved and cared for place of worship.

After looking around and absorbing the peaceful atmosphere, I noticed a sign above a donation box which said: 'The Lord loveth a cheerful giver.'

'Oh does he indeed,' I said, grinning broadly at Muriel whilst groping for my purse.

But before I had time to insert my donation I tripped over an unnoticed obstacle and went sprawling, spilling the contents of my purse all over the floor.

As I lay there, momentarily stunned, Muriel did not seem unduly concerned at my predicament, but knowing my propensity for swearing when I hurt myself, urgently cried out, 'No profanity in the church – *please!*'

I spared the Lord the profanity, but neither of us was able to stifle the uncontrollable giggling that followed my mishap and her reaction to it.

On leaving the church I turned to Muriel and said, 'Well at least we've proved to the Lord that we *are* "cheerful givers.

WHAT ABOUT THE OTHERS?

I never had a special friend when I was at St. Anne's Home, but this was from choice as, although I tried to be friendly with everyone, there was no one I particularly wished to befriend. There were, however, a few of the younger children, apart from my sister, who I cared about.

One of these was a child called Miriam who came to St. Anne's about two years after me. She was a poor wretch of a child who was constantly in trouble with Matron Calcutt, not so much because she was deliberately naughty but she could never quite grasp what was expected of her.

She cried a lot in frustration and sometimes wet herself and her punishment on at least two occasions, was to be stripped naked and frog-marched into the back yard next to the laundry, where some of the older girls were ordered to throw buckets of cold water over her to "clean her up and teach her a lesson." After one of these appalling punishments she became so distraught that when no one was looking she took a pair of sewing scissors and stabbed herself in the eye. She was sent away after that and we never saw her again.

Winnie Botton, about the same age as me, joined the ATS and was posted to an ack-ack army unit to try and shoot down enemy aircraft. Rachel Powell married a Catholic man when she was sixteen and I think she had eight children. Other than that I have no idea what happened to the others.

However, the most famous person who was at St. Anne's for a short spell (though not in my time but my sister's) was one - Jennifer Schumacher. She was there because apparently her mother was suffering a long illness. She was a stunningly attractive girl with a charming, kindly manner and, according to my sister, very popular with all the girls and they were sorry when she went back home after her mother's eventual recovery. She married very young and as 'Jennifer Chimes' became Miss Great Britain, followed by Miss England and then runner up in the Miss World contest. She divorced her husband and subsequently married the comedian Max Wall. The marriage didn't last and she eventually married a solicitor and settled to a quiet life in the Warwickshire countryside.

CELIA

There was one person however, who'd been an inmate of St. Anne's (though again, not in my time) whose story, I feel, is worth telling. Her name was Celia Taylor (nee Hamilton) and she came to me for a job as a Rep. at the firm of which I was the manager. She was a tall, good looking woman, whose features were often marred by the troubled look she frequently wore. I gave her the job because, during the interview, when I asked about her educational achievements she said she had none, mentioning she'd spent her life either in foster care or various institutions all over the place, finally ending up at St. Anne's Home. I didn't tell her of my connection, but gave her the job as I wanted to give her a chance.

She was married with three children to a man called Bart Taylor, whom I knew *of*, but didn't *know*, although I believed him to be a bit of a rough diamond who was a dealer in antiques, horses and second-hand cars, and whose work premises were under some railway arches in a less salubrious place at the lower end of town.

She turned out to be a very good worker and when I got to know her better she confided in me about her life and how, when she was at St. Anne's, although Mrs. Legge (the then matron) did her best to help her with her problems, it didn't stop her running away from time to time. I asked her where she ran to and she said she often broke into any one of the cars at the railway arches she could get into and slept in it. One day Bart found her asleep in a car when he came to work and took her back to St. Anne's. She didn't run away again, but when she was sixteen she went to the arches to see him. He eventually married her and they settled in a nice little house in Warwick where one would suppose they could live happily ever after.

But she was still not a happy person and after getting to know her a little better she confided in me something of her background. It transpired she had been fostered when she was a baby and never knew who her parents were. Thereafter, for as far back as she could remember, she had been in and out of foster homes and children's homes and always felt that wherever she was she was never wanted and had run away, eventually ending up at St. Anne's.

She desperately wanted to find out who her mother was and one day, when there was no one about, managed to sneak into matron's office at the Home and rifle through a filing cabinet until she found her dossier. It gave her mother's name followed by the statement, "Mother prostitute, father unknown." This only served to make her feel even less happy, for she then thought it would have been better to have kept her illusions rather than be burdened with such an unsavoury piece of knowledge.

When she told me this I advised her not to give up – she had her mother's name and that was a start. After many enquiries and set-backs, she eventually discovered that her mother had two sisters who ran a tea shop in a small town in Sussex, but she still could find no trace of her mother. So she decided to telephone the tea shop, but when she said, 'My name is Celia and I believe your sister is my mother,' they made no answer and put the phone down. At this point she felt she'd gone as far as she could go and gave up in despair.

Then one day she came into my office and asked if she could talk to me. 'You'll never believe this,' she said, but Saturday afternoon a man came into the antique shop when I happened to be there looking for a certain item.'

She said she explained to him that they hadn't got what he was looking for in stock but asked him to call in again as these things did turn up from time to time. But he explained that it was doubtful if he'd be this way again anytime soon, as he lived in Sussex and went on to name the little town in which he lived which, by an extraordinary coincidence, happened to be the very same town where her mother's sisters had the tea shop.

Astounded by this happenstance, she poured out her story to him and he said, 'Give me your name and details of where you can be reached. I use that tea shop quite often, so leave it with me.'

She didn't hold out any hope that anything would come of it until one day, some months later, she came into my office, all smiles and handed me a letter saying, 'Would you read this when you have time?'

It was from her mother! I read it and discovered that her mother, far from being a prostitute, was a civil servant who had moved to South Africa after the war to work in the Colonial Service, where she met and married her husband - another British civil servant - and they spent the rest of their working lives there. They were now retired, had recently moved back to this country and were living in Northampton.

After all these years it is difficult for me to remember all the details in the letter but the gist of it was that the mother was thrilled to have found her daughter and when could they meet.

So a meeting was arranged. Celia drove to Northampton on the given day, but rather than go to her mother's home, she felt it would be better if they met on neutral ground, so they decided on The Park Café in Abington Park, Northampton.

When Celia got back she told me all about it. She'd arrived at the café much earlier than the time arranged, so after ordering a coffee, she stuck her head in a book to take her mind off her nervousness and while away the waiting. Each time someone entered, she looked up and each time decided: No – that's not her, or, oh dear, I hope *that's* not her

Then she became temporarily engrossed in what she was reading and didn't notice anyone come in until she was aware that someone was approaching her table. She looked up and there, standing before her was a woman who was older, but otherwise an exact replica of herself. The meeting was joyful and emotional and Celia listened as her mother explained the circumstances of her birth and why she'd had to give her up. She was very young and living at home with her family in Brighton. It was war time and she met a soldier with whom she'd fallen in love. She became pregnant, but when she told him, instead of saying he would marry her, he said he couldn't help her as he was already married and she never saw him again. When Celia was born the parents said that she would not be allowed to bring the shame of an illegitimate baby into the family and she must give the baby up or leave home. The choice was stark but she finally agreed that Celia could be fostered, rather than adopted.

And so began Celia's life in numerous foster homes and children's homes, in none of which she was happy and from many of which she ran away.

But now, at last, here was the happy ending she thought she'd never find, to a truly sad story… Or was it?

I was invited to meet the mother and her husband when they came on a visit to Leamington. We all went for a meal at one of the local hotels and I found them both agreeable and pleasant, although I did wonder why the mother also looked a little sad at times and put it down to the years she'd missed with her daughter and the fact that she'd never had another child. I also thought it strange that Celia's husband and children were not included in the gathering, or even mentioned.

Back in the work place, although I was pleased for Celia's new found happiness, I eventually had to warn her that the time had come when she would have to choose between her job and her mother, as she was taking too much time off work to make frequent visits to her. I also said I felt her first duty should be to her husband and children, whom she confessed she'd thought of leaving so that she could be with her mother all the time.

She then, between tears, said she loved her mother like no one she'd ever loved before, but despite the fact that she showered her with gifts and flowers and chocolates her mother had become cool and unresponsive. 'I've been rejected yet again,' she sobbed.

Rightly or wrongly, my sympathies lay with the mother, and since Celia was confiding in me and asking my advice, I told to grow up, back off her mother a bit, and give more time and love to her husband and children, who needed her love as much as she needed her mother's love. I also told her that if she continued taking time off work I'd have no option but to ask her to leave. She flounced off in a huff, then returned a bit later to say she was sorry, but she thought she would leave anyway and we parted on fairly amicable terms.

Then I had a phone call from her mother asking if there was any possibility of my giving Celia her job back. I had to refuse, saying I'd already replaced her. 'Oh dear,' said her mother. I'm really at my wits end.'

She then confided that Celia was spending so much time at her home that it had now become an embarrassment. It was also causing a rift between her and her husband and she didn't quite know how to resolve the situation without causing too much hurt. She was also concerned about Celia's own marriage.

I didn't really feel I could be of much help and began to wish I'd never become involved, but suggested she tried using a bit of tough love and tell her that in spending so much time with her she was neglecting her own family who need would be greater.

The next time I saw Celia was when I bumped into her some months later. She looked an absolute wreck; told me she was recovering from a nervous breakdown and when I enquired after her mother she said she and her husband had gone back to live in South Africa as the British climate didn't suit them. She also told me that she and her husband had sold up and bought a farm in Wales to which they would shortly be moving. I wished her well and went on my way.

But that was not the end of the story. Several years later, I was waiting in the doctor's surgery at Talgarth when I noticed a young woman who kept looking at me. Eventually, she gave me a shy smile and spoke. 'Excuse me,' she said, 'did you used to live in Leamington Spa?'

I averred that I did, but asked her how she knew.

'My mother used to work for you', she said.

'Oh, and who was your mother?' I enquired.

'Celia Taylor,' she said.

'Well fancy you recognising me after all this time,' I replied in astonishment, especially as I hadn't even remembered ever meeting any of Celia's children. I then added, 'How is your mother?'

'She's dead,' she said flatly, without any sign of sorrow.

'Oh dear,' I said sympathetically. 'You must miss her dreadfully.'

'No, we don't,' she said with surprising candidness. 'She was horrible to us when we were kids, always going off and leaving us to fend for ourselves. And when she was there she made our lives a misery and would beat us up for the least little thing.'

After we'd fulfilled our surgery appointments I spoke further with her and she told me her mother had died of cancer but neither she nor her siblings were sorry at her passing. Her father was living alone on the farm they'd moved to when they left the Midlands.

On parting she gave me her email address and asked me if I would keep in touch, but I saw no reason to and lost the bit of paper.

Thinking about the conversation afterwards I found it extraordinary that someone who had suffered throughout her childhood in the way Celia had, would have done her best to make sure her own children were loved and happy. There is just no explaining the vagaries of human behaviour.

NO REST IN PEACE

I once had an uneasy friendship with a person called Connie, who was something of a hypochondriac – always at the doctor's surgery demanding a cure for some trivial, real or imagined illness.

On one occasion when I met her I said brightly, 'Hello Connie, are you well?' to which she severely replied, 'I am *never* well. Some days I am better than others but I am *never* well!'

It was rumoured that the doctors were fed-up with her many and varied illnesses and passed her from one to another until finally, the only one who agreed to see her was an elderly doctor who was not far off retirement. He had become rather forthright in his old age and told her he didn't want to see her again for another three months, by which time he knew he would no longer be in practice.

In the meantime, Connie died and the elderly doctor felt very guilty, but his guilt didn't last long for shortly after, he died himself and, coincidentally, they were buried in plots next to each other in the local cemetery.

Then a joke began to circulate and I swear it wasn't me who made it up. It goes: "Not long after he'd been buried the doctor thought he heard a persistent tapping on his coffin. 'Good God!' he cried irritably, 'Who is it? I'm supposed to be enjoying eternal rest in peace.'

'Sorry to bother you doctor, it's only me,' said Connie. 'You told me to see you in three months so here I am. Do you have a cure for worms?'

MARY

Yesterday, I found myself wandering in the sunlit woodlands of my early days, where bluebells and stitchwort, primroses and wood anemone, wood sorrel and red campion all vied for my admiration.

Lured by the sound of the unseen brook, I sauntered down to the banks and watched the silvered waters tumbling purposefully on to an unknown destination, never to pass this way again. I reached up to take a large leaf from an alder tree and curled it into a fairy cup, then as I stooped to fill it with water, I became aware of another presence. I looked up and there, like a misted mirage, stood Mary. She drew nearer and I could see she was all smiles and full of youthful vigour, which was surprising, since the last time I saw her, her legs were swollen and bound in bandages to control the oedematous weeping

We were curiously incurious as to why we should both be where we were, but seized the moment and lay down on the bank together to squint up through the filigreed traceries of the leaves of the silver birch, and marvel at the intense blue of the late spring sky. Lowering my eyes from my ecstatic gaze, I looked down to my left to see an army of ants swarming over the gently decaying trunk of a fallen tree.

Not wishing to risk the torment of itching skin from ant bites, we left our mossy mattresses and strolled further into the woodlands until I became tired and refused to walk any further. Mary said she must keep walking for she still had a long way to go, then gave me one of her enigmatic smiles and disappeared as mysteriously as she had appeared.

* * * * * *

When I woke up, instead of the usual, half-remembered, tattered fragments of a dream, it was still vivid and I felt an irrepressible urge to telephone Mary as soon as the time was decently acceptable.

Several intermittent phone calls brought no response, so I drove the few miles to visit her. She was not at home so I went to see one of her six daughters who lived near.

'She's in hospital,' said Adelaide. 'She had a stroke last night.'

On my way home I felt unutterably sad and reflected: how strange it is that our dreams so often paint a picture that is the complete reverse of reality, and even stranger, that when I saw her in the woods, full of smiles and youthful vigour, may well have been somewhere about the time she'd had her stroke.

She died a few days later, but my abiding memory of her will be as she appeared to me in my dream. And I remembered some short pieces of prose she'd written to me some years previously and I print them here as a tribute to her memory.

AN AUTUMN MORNING
November 2006

The weather slot on the radio forecast more rain for the coming day. It was early morning, just getting light. Standing by the window I mused that we had had enough rain really. Everywhere was sodden and the wind had been gusting fiercely. At least that had stopped. So, another gloomy, cast-over day, with low cloud over the hills and mist curling through Hay Forest.

It was over an hour later that I stood in the same place, looking out of the same window. Now, through the trees of the wood on the eastern side of the front window, the sun's light was strengthening.

Clouds there were, certainly, coming from the west. But they met the sun's oblique rays, which turned and held them pink, against a sky which for now was clear. Low strands of cloud underneath Hay Forest, and the wall of the hills softened into dove grey, no longer threatening.

Centre stage, the sun turned every tree and bush which showed autumn colour into a brightness of green, gold and yellow. All was transformed and radiant now, as I watched the young birch trees tremulously shake their sparkling silver leaves.

To see bright beauty like this on an early autumn morning is magical indeed. We know if we climb a certain hill there'll be a spectacular view. It is expected. But nature will always be putting on the style, as on this particular morning. We are privileged if we have time to stand and stare, and catch these enchanting moments.

PRESSURE IS A PRIVILEGE
(Title of a book by Billie-Jean King)
From Mary to Lynn - Summer 2006

Lynn has a nice line in being on the side of angels. She proclaims, as we drive over The Begwyns, 'I consider myself privileged to live in such a beautiful part of the country with such spectacular views extending in whichever direction the eye cares to wander.'

I murmur something in agreement, but nothing will sound so nicely satisfying, or reflect so well the benign smile of the Almighty as the silent, heartfelt and all embracing peace experienced in the vastness and beauty of our surroundings.

When back to the hurly-burley and reality of everyday existence, she will declare, with the same fervour as she extols the virtues of peace and tranquillity, "Pressure is a privilege – live with it!'

This maxim seems to be directed especially at people like me, who strive earnestly to live without it, and try to bat it off as soon as it looms.

But there we are. Lynn will adjust her stance in the cause of achieving her object in, for her, so small a thing as a luncheon date.

'No pressure,' she'll say, as she claims our attendance. 'No pressure,' while awaiting our acquiescence.

Darling Lynn – I love and enjoy your pressure and privilege in whatever form it comes.

From a useless, admiring adherent.

You were a good friend Mary – I shall miss you.

1930 - 2016

WHAT PRICE FREEDOM

This was my choice
To cherish my freedom.
The freedom to do what I wanted
When, and with whom.
This freedom was very precious.
Friends wanted to know me,
Sought my company;
Thought they needed me.
But I danced to my own tune,
Dripped charm, scattered favours
Like confetti floating on a breeze –
Flattered, and withdrew

Do not come close…

 I belonged to everyone
Yet owned by no one,
Admired and desired –

But do not come too close…

Now suddenly I am old and tired,
Popularity long expired.
The flotsam of forgotten dreams
Where nothing is but what it seems.

Come a little closer…

And tell me: what price then
This freedom I once held so dear.
Now that I no longer value it –
Who will buy?

THE PERENNIAL GIFT

Today is one of my good days and I want
to do something special -
but what can I do?
I want to sing sweetly and joyfully,
but I am old and my voice
has become uncertain and tuneless.
I want to skip and dance
amongst the daisies on the lawn,
but my legs are heavy
and my knees stiff with age.
I want to capture the beauty of a flower
by painting a picture, but have not the skill.
I want to write a lovely poem,
but the words will not flow.
I want to do all these things,
but you know, and I know, that I cannot.
So I will content myself
by listening to others sing;
watching the children skip and dance;
looking at wonderful works of art
and reading the beautiful poems of the poets.
And I will give thanks to you Lord,
for granting me the perennial -
Gift of Appreciation.

LOST CAUSE

Turning out the drawers
In anticipation of the inevitable,
Agonising over what to keep
And what to discard –
My eyes are drawn to a
Tarnished old medal lurking in a corner.

Picking it up, I turn it over;
On the reverse side it reads:
"Ladies hundred yards sprint champion 1954"
I tossed it back in the drawer,
Retrieved it, cast it away once more.

And wondered:
How had this medal survived
All previous purges on relics
Of past endeavour.

Looking back, how could I ever
Have thought in life the only aim –
Another gong, a bit more fame.
Get to your marks, wait for the gun…
Another race that must be won.

All past glories long forgot –
They matter not a single jot…

Where did I toss that tarnished medal?
Perhaps I'll keep it after all.
A worthless thing, but just a small
Reminder that I haven't always been
The frail, dithering old bat
That now I seem.

CHRONIC PROBLEM

I had been beset by a few health problems which put me out of circulation for a short spell. When I felt well enough to face the world again a friend said, 'Hello. I haven't seen you for a few weeks. Are you well?'

Feeling anything but, I nevertheless gave the stock reply, 'Yes, I'm fine thank you.'

He looked a little puzzled, then said, 'I'm glad to hear it, only someone told me you'd been in hospital. What's been the problem?'

'Well, since you ask,' I said, 'I have polymialgia, pernicious anaemia, a dodgy heart and an indomitable spirit.'

'Ah! Good news,' he said. 'The first three things can be treated but nothing to be done about the fourth.'

THE UNWELCOME TRUTH

There's nothing like a painfully honest nephew to remind one of one's mortality. I was recently having a telephone conversation with him and misunderstood something he said.

Anxious not to let him think he was at fault I said, 'Oh dear – I'm so sorry – I think I must be cracking up.'

'Don't worry,' he said soothingly. 'After all, people of your age are not only cracking up – they're usually decomposing.'

THE LAST LAUGH

Since I am very, very old I can say impossibly outrageous things (which I would never have dreamt of saying when I was young) and get away with it.

Our chaste Parish Priest, who sometimes winds me up with a bit of racy banter, came to see me when I was languishing in hospital recovering from a heart attack.

I gave him a mischievous smile and said, 'Well, what have you come for – to give me the kiss of life, or to administer the last rites?'

'Both,' he replied, 'which would you like first?'

MY FAVOURITE PRAYER

O Lord, support us all the day long

throughout this troublous life,

until the shades lengthen,

the evening comes,

the busy world is hushed,

the fever of life is over

and our work is done.

Then in thy great mercy,

grant us safe lodging, a

holy rest and peace at the last.

MY OWN MANTRA

Thank you Lord for this day,

for all my yesterdays

and for the days that are yet to come.

Previous work by the same author.

A LIFE IS WHAT YOU GET
can be bought from Amazon by typing in the author's name:
Lynn M. Trowbridge or directly from the author
Email:l.trowbridge23@btinternet .com.